THE TRUMPET CALL

About the Author

Lorna Bourdeaux studied German and Russian before joining the staff of Keston College, a research centre, which studies and publishes information about all aspects of religious life in Eastern Europe and the Soviet Union. In her role as research assistant she has travelled extensively, gaining first-hand information on oppression of individuals where such problems persist.

She is married to Michael, who is Director of Keston College. They live in Kent.

Valeri Barinov

THE TRUMPET CALL

Lorna Bourdeaux

Marshalls

Marshalls Paperbacks
Marshall Pickering
3 Beggarwood Lane, Basingstoke, Hants, RG23 7LP, UK
A subsidiary of the Zondervan Corporation

First published in 1985 by Marshall Morgan & Scott Ltd.

Keston Book Number 21

British Library CIP data

Bourdeaux, Lorna
    Valeri Barinov: the trumpet call.
    1. Barinov, Valeri   2. Prisoners—Soviet
    Union—Biography
    I. Title
    365'.45'0947   HV9713

ISBN 0–551–01297–8

Phototypeset by Input Typesetting Ltd, London
Printed in Great Britain by Anchor Brendon Ltd, Tiptree, Essex

Extracts from the book *Nomenklatura* by Michael Voslensky are
reprinted by kind permission of the publishers, The Bodley
Head Ltd. Extracts from *Inside the Soviet Army* by Viktor
Suvorov are reprinted by kind permission of the author and the
publishers, Hamish Hamilton. Extracts from *Red and Hot* by S.
Frederick Starr are reprinted by kind permission of the
publishers, Oxford University Press.

To Michael

Acknowledgements

I would like to express my warmest thanks to members of staff at Keston College who helped with translating and transcribing materials from Russian and checking the manuscript including, Mike Rowe, Alyona Kojevnikov and Marite Sapiets. Special thanks to Caroline Andrews who typed the whole manuscript and was a constant source of encouragement; to Britta Saffran who did so much to help run my household while I was writing; to my husband, Michael, for advice and encouragement; to several friends, both in the UK and abroad, who contributed the various 'testimonies'.

Contents

Foreword

By Cliff Richard

My only visit to the Soviet Union was back in '76 for a concert tour.

It was a strange experience in some ways and my recollections tend to be of drab surroundings and subdued, controlled atmospheres.

The one exception was an encounter with a bunch of young Christians from a place called Tallinn. They'd heard I was playing in Leningrad and despite having no show tickets they crammed into a battered old mini bus and drove the 9-hour journey determined somehow to make contact. Happily for me they did and we managed to squeeze them into the hall around the sound desk. The next day we met in my hotel room and they explained why my visit to their country was so important for them. It was nothing to do with the music or starry-eyed fan worship, that was for sure. What mattered was that I was a Christian and that I wasn't scared or ashamed to say so from the stage.

It was the first time, according to these youngsters, that any visiting 'celebrity' had publicly stood up for Jesus, and they were just over the moon about it. For a little while they were able to emerge from their secret 'underground church' situation and be part of an atmosphere where Jesus was freely, enthusiastically and genuinely acknowledged. I would never realise, they told me, just what an encouragement that was.

I share that memory because although I've never met Valeri Barinov, I feel an affinity with him which stems largely, I know, from what I learned from those Tallinn Christians. It's much more than our mutual enjoyment of rock music – although that's part of it. The real affinity comes from belonging to the same Christian Family as Valeri, and consequently identifying in a way with his hurts, frustrations and persecution. I guess it took that Soviet encounter to show me a glimpse of how far the implications and responsibilities of Family membership actually extend.

This book is sure to be an enormous boost to Valeri and probably to a whole host of other Soviet Christians who are struggling to survive amid isolation and persecution. What I suspect too is that the story of Valeri's courage and faithfulness will sting some of us more 'comfortable' Christians who jog along, complacent and unthinking about our freedom, into more determined 'up front' Christian living and witness.

Cliff Richard
June 1985

Introduction

By the Rt. Hon David Steel MP

I first visited the Soviet Union as a student in 1959. The cold, drab and colourless impression first gained of Soviet cities and people at that time stood in stark contrast to the warm, sharp vitality of the individual citizens when one had the opportunity to talk to them. Here is a nation which is proud, intensely patriotic, and yet also lively, fun-loving and bubbling with goodwill towards their fellow human beings. The problem: they are denied the basic human rights – to move freely, to congregate freely, to speak freely and to choose those who govern them – which no government has the right to deny. When I visited Russia again in January 1984 I found the appearance of the cities and their inhabitants much changed. Superficially there has been a great improvement in the standard of living and the colourfulness of the place. Underneath, this vibrant nation is still senselessly repressed.

Valeri Barinov, through his admirable courage in sacrificing everything for his beliefs, is the conscience of the oppressed Soviet peoples. As a rock musician and as a Christian he is doubly dangerous in the eyes of the Soviet authorities – because his message to young people is doubly powerful. Yet the authorities are ironically impotent against him. Unable to convict him on a criminal charge they can only declare him insane. They may, with their infernal tortures, break his mind. They will not break his message.

In my twenty years as a Member of Parliament I have held the belief that conditions in the Soviet Union can only improve if we succeed in reducing world tension. Soviet actions have been motivated as much by fear of what they perceive to be a hostile western world as by communist doctrine. Let us not forget that Russia suffered horribly in two world wars in this century. But while we seek to open contacts at government level and to work patiently through a dialogue we must never cease to draw attention to our deep disapproval of the way in which human freedoms are crushed. Backed up by unstinting protest by individuals in the West, much can be achieved for the victims of repression.

Keston College plays an invaluable role in keeping alight the candle of hope for Soviet prisoners. Lorna Bourdeaux's tireless work in producing this book, which contains extensive first-hand information obtained from Valeri Barinov's papers and correspondence, deserves the thanks and the admiration of all of us. Valeri Barinov preaches a powerful Christian message, but this book will appeal to an audience far beyond the membership of the Christian family.

I commend it to you.

David Steel
August 1985

1: God's red cross

With a team of doctors inside, the ambulance gathered pace. Traffic and pedestrians scattered before it and the long vista of the Nevsky Prospekt opened out ahead. The driver laughed at the power of his own speed, telling the doctors that God would see them to the scene of the accident and they were all safe in God's hands.

So many industrial disasters happened these days and they were sure this was a bad one: the collapse of a building under construction. In the few minutes between the call at the depot and arrival at the scene the doctors were anxiously preparing themselves to do their work, but this driver challenged them with the name of God, telling them that he would be watching over them while they tried to save lives.

These doctors had never heard a sermon before and least expected it while on call, but Valeri Barinov rarely missed an opportunity to present others with a testimony about his belief in God.

Having a red cross on the side of his vehicle appealed to Valeri as a Christian symbol in a society which officially rejected God. It was a good starting point for a conversation with anyone he drove. Not even Valeri could take the New Testament out of his pocket and preach from it while driving at breakneck speed, but he often gave the impression that he was about to try. There were even occasions of waiting at the scene of an accident when the Bible could be used to comfort the injured. Even if no one was actually converted as a result of Valeri's witness during these moments of intense activity, seeds were sown and this was not the time to mock the driver.

Valeri's ambulance was not equipped to carry the victims back to hospital, so his contact was always more with the doctors and nurses than with the patients, but most of the medical profession who rode in Valeri's ambulance remembered the occasion. Few people failed to respond to the warmth of his personality even if they did not accept his message.

Later, as Valeri drove away from the chaotic scene on the building site, leaving the medical team to attend to the injured, he rejoiced inwardly that once again he had been given the opportunity to share his faith.

His next task was to make a brief detour on the way back to the ambulance depot to deliver a message to two English students who were studying in Leningrad, whom he had met a couple of weeks previously at the Leningrad Baptist Church. The two girls were living at the hostel at Mytninskaya Naberezhnaya, across the Neva from the beautiful Hermitage Museum. He slipped into the building and hastily pinned a folded piece of paper on to the notice board. The message, in Russian, read: 'Tonight at 7.30 p.m. at the Lunokhod (Moon Walker). Please come to see Tanya and the children first and have supper with us. Pray for our group, that the Lord will give us an opportunity to speak about him. Your Brother in Christ, Valeri.'

That evening Valeri 'borrowed' his ambulance from the depot to go on quite a different mission. He had to pick up a set of drums, amplifiers, three electric guitars, an electric organ and all the electrical paraphernalia that went with this equipment, from various friends scattered around the city. He transported it all to the local communist youth club, the Lunokhod, about ten minutes' walk from his home. As he arrived and started to unload the gear, the other members of his small, amateur rock group, Igor, Vova, Sasha and Sergei, turned up. They were all in their late teens or early twenties, at least ten years younger than Valeri, but they regarded him as a close friend and confidant and had enormous respect for him. None of them was a Christian, but they knew that for

Valeri his faith was central to his whole life and they could not help being affected by it. Whenever they spent time with him, the conversation inevitably turned to spiritual matters.

But on that particular evening they were all preoccupied with setting up their equipment quickly, so that they could rehearse a new Paul McCartney number which they had been practising throughout the previous week. Although the amplification system was ancient and their instruments of poor quality, they took their music very seriously, not least because the local kids, most of them still at school, were a very discerning audience. They avidly collected and swopped records of Western pop groups and recorded songs from Western radio broadcasts, so they knew what the songs were supposed to sound like. Valeri and the group had won great popularity locally and they didn't want to disappoint their young fans.

For the English girls this was the first time they had been to a disco 'Russian style' and they watched with growing curiosity as groups of young people arrived, chatting, laughing and greeting each other with obvious enthusiasm. They urged the group to get on with the music and soon everyone was dancing with little sign of self-consciousness. They could have been a group of young people anywhere in the West except for their hairstyles and clothing. What the Western visitors had heard about the Soviet Union being ten years out of date appeared to be true. This was 1977, but the girls were still wearing skirts well above their knees. The boys all wore their hair over their collars. But there was a lack of individuality in their outward appearance. Items of clothing which are mass-produced in Soviet factories have a tendency to look like the components of a uniform. For these kids, the way they dressed had little to do with the whims of fashion. Clothing was a matter of utility and availability.

As the dancers gyrated to the music, Valeri grinned and sang, using his body as an extra instrument of the band. He knew a whole repertoire of old Beatles songs for which he had learned the English lyrics. The other members of the group joined in the vocals with a mixture of English and Russian and a good many indistinguishable utterances! After about an hour Valeri and the group took a break and went outside the club into the night air to cool down.

When they re-entered the hall the buzz of voices rose to a new pitch of excitement. They knew that in the second half the group would perform some new songs. Valeri took a microphone in his hand and there was a sudden hush as everyone waited for him to announce the next number. But to the amazement of the two English visitors and probably everyone else except the members of the group, Valeri put his hand in his back pocket and drew out a small, well-thumbed New Testament. 'Before we sing again, I want to read a few verses from God's holy word so that you can think about them in the coming week.' He read from one of Paul's epistles and then gave a short impassioned exposition of the verses. The young people listened with complete attention, unable to take their eyes away from Valeri's face which was transfigured with joy as he spoke. It was difficult to gauge their reaction from their faces because they betrayed hardly any emotion, but Valeri's words gripped them. After he had finished speaking Valeri simply turned to the members of the group, grinning as he made a thumbs-up sign, and played a few chords on his guitar as a signal for them to resume.

It was nearly midnight by the time Valeri was actually on his way home, having delivered all the pieces of equipment to their respective owners, dropped the ambulance at the depot and waited for the tram. He was delighted with the success of the evening. He had felt the Holy Spirit's presence with him prompting him to share the Gospel with the young people. He thanked God in his heart that there had been no vigilantes prowling around outside the club – he would have been in serious trouble by now if they had heard what he had said after the interval. As he closed his eyes with weariness he could see some of the intense young faces in his mind's eye. How he longed for them to become Christians. He offered up a silent prayer, knowing that the seeds of faith had been planted in some of their hearts. He had obeyed the prompting of the Holy Spirit and now the future of those young souls rested with the Lord. Yes, today had been an eventful one and Valeri rejoiced that now he could go home to rest knowing that he had put God first in everything and that great blessing would follow.

As for me – one of the two English girls – that particular memory of Valeri is one that I shall always treasure. Despite the suffering and deprivation which he is enduring at this very moment in a Soviet prison camp, I cannot help feeling that the same joy and confidence which he radiated to the doctors in the ambulance, the members of his first rock band, the young people at the Lunokhod and countless others will also touch the hearts of his embittered prison inmates and the hardened prison camp personnel, and that even there the seeds of faith will be sown in people's hearts.

2: From vodka to God

Valeri Alexandrovich Barinov was born on 6th December, 1944 in Leningrad. His parents lived in a communal flat in a decaying residential suburb called Trinity Fields in the south-west of the city. Their marriage was an unhappy one and they separated soon after Valeri was born, so he was brought up entirely by his mother until her death in 1956 when he was eleven years old. Although Valeri has written very little about his mother, his memories of her are happy ones.* He describes her as a very good woman with many friends who devoted herself wholeheartedly to his upbringing. He does not tell us the cause of her death which followed a serious illness, but indicates that she suffered great mental anxiety as a result of her unhappy marriage.

One way in which Valeri's mother significantly influenced her son's life in the short time that was available to her was by identifying and encouraging his musical talents. From the age of six she sent him to violin lessons at the school attached to the Rimsky-Korsakov Conservatoire in Leningrad. He excelled in all his examinations and everything seemed to augur well for his admission to the school at the Conservatoire for a specialist education. However, this proved to be impossible. We do not know exactly why, but Valeri indicates that his mother's sudden illness prevented him from entering the school. In retrospect, Valeri sees this event as God's first direct intervention in his life.

* In this chapter all the quotations are taken from materials written or recorded by Valeri Barinov.

If he had been able to take advantage of a good musical education, it is likely that he would have become a professional musician with every prospect of making a good career. 'That had to be denied me', wrote Valeri, 'because otherwise I would have been devoted, not to doing God's will, but to following my own career.' Although this outcome was not Valeri's own choice and he was not a Christian at the time, his words are relevant to thousands of Christians in the Soviet Union today and describe their situation very aptly. The attempts by the Soviet authorities systematically to deny higher education to people who openly profess religious belief make it extremely difficult for them to enter any of the professions. For the majority of Christians, only the most menial jobs are available which give no scope for their creative energy or practical ability. As a result, they devote their unused talents, both intellectual and practical, to the service of God and the church. In Valeri's case the opportunity did come, much later, to use his God-given musical talent in preaching the gospel.

Bereft of both parents, he was placed under the guardianship of his mother's brother. Valeri refers only very briefly to that period of his childhood which was obviously a very unhappy one. His uncle drank heavily and was often violent. Valeri frequently ran away and spent the nights on the streets. Eventually he was placed in a state boarding school. It was probably at this stage that Valeri first realised that he was going to have to use all his own resources to advance himself. In the Soviet system, which is dominated entirely by a privileged ruling élite, it is very hard to make a good career and enjoy material prosperity unless you have the right connections. In this respect, Valeri was at a grave disadvantage, although he did not fully realise this until much later in life.

At school he was hardworking and cheerful and with his outgoing personality he made friends easily and always entered into communal activities with enthusiasm. He had no further opportunity to study the violin, but in the meantime he had developed a very good voice and always took part in school singing groups, often performing solo roles. He describes himself at that time as being full of youthful idealism and intensely patriotic. 'I was a very active pupil and from 1958–9 I served on a battleship as an apprentice, a ship's boy. In 1959 at the end of my service I was even the leader of a section of the ship. If someone had told me to give my life for my country, I would have been prepared to do so.' Valeri gives no details about how he managed to get this apprenticeship at the age of fourteen or what exactly he did after he had completed it, but he does indicate that in his late teens his idealism began to pall and he gradually became aware of all kinds of injustice in the society in which he was living. He does not give any examples, but perhaps he was simply finding out that it is not necessarily those who are hardworking and honest who can expect to do well, but rather those with least integrity, who know how to manipulate others for their own ends. 'I was sensitive and so naturally I took in what was going on around me and stored it all up inwardly. But on the surface I didn't take any notice because there were people who stood up for me. Somehow at that time the injustice didn't seem so blatant.'

After he had become a Christian, Valeri's greatest desire was to help young people who, like him, became aware of injustice during their formative years, but had no moral principles to guide them in their dilemma. He befriended many young people who were themselves the victims of injustice – many were juvenile delinquents – and presented the Gospel to them as the only solution to their problems.

It took many years, however, before Valeri himself discovered how to live a Christian life. In his late teens Valeri began to rebel against society. Deprived of the stability and emotional security of a normal family life, he became increasingly reckless in his behaviour. He was thrown out of a number of jobs before 1963 when he was called up to do military service in the Soviet army. This event coincided with another very significant one which was eventually to change the whole course of his life.

Before he left for the army his mother's sister, Tamara Dmitrievna Pronina, told him about her firm personal belief in the existence of God. Probably Valeri had heard his aunt talk about God before, but he had never really listened and even on this occasion he tried to dismiss such thoughts from his mind. Valeri wrote, referring to his aunt: 'There you are, such a young person and already in the ranks of the elderly.* But you know, a doctor is an educated person. Of course, I didn't laugh about people's feelings and convictions but this apparent contradiction – young, educated and a believer – gave me the impetus to search for God.' His aunt's words – 'God exists' – were what he carried with him in his subconscious as he left his familiar environment in Leningrad to begin a new life in the army.

Valeri describes himself at that time in the following way: 'When I was a youth before call-up age I could not say that Christ was risen: no God whatsoever existed as far as I was concerned. In school I was taught there is no God. There were no Bibles on sale anywhere; on the contrary, there were only atheist brochures. I must be honest, I wasn't remotely interested in such questions.'

Valeri was conditioned like every other Soviet child, from the age of seven when he entered school, to believe that all religion was merely an anachronism, a remnant of a bourgeois ideology, and that religious belief in the countries of 'progressive socialism' was rapidly disappearing from people's hearts and minds. Soviet propaganda would like everyone to believe this, but there is much evidence to the contrary. After nearly seven decades in power, the Communist Party of the Soviet Union has still not succeeded in eradicating religious belief and there is evidence of great spiritual revival in all branches of religion and particularly in all Christian denominations.

If the Soviet rulers are to have any measure of success in their campaign to get rid of religion, they must obviously

* Soviet propaganda constantly reiterates the falsehood that only old women go to church.

concentrate their main efforts on the minds of young people. I want briefly to fill out the background to Valeri's story and describe this process of indoctrination and to indicate what, in the absence of a morality based on Christian ethics or any other religious moral code, constitutes the basis, in theory at least, of socialist morality.

From the day a child first enters kindergarten at the age of three or four Lenin becomes a major factor in his school life. When one walks through the streets of Moscow or Leningrad, one is confronted, on nearly every street corner, with huge portraits of Lenin and in a Soviet child's world, in the classroom, the corridor, even the playground, there are smiling portraits of 'Uncle Lenin'. Children are taught to recognise and respect Lenin's portrait, they lay flowers on statues of the great man, they sing songs about him which depict him as the best human being who ever lived. Soviet children react to him with a mixture of awe and affection which among Western children is reserved for Father Christmas or the infant Jesus. Indeed, Lenin becomes an object of veneration and children are rewarded for their zeal in treating him as such.

Discipline, patriotism and a sense of collective responsibility are fostered by a succession of children's and youth organisations: the Octobrists, the Young Pioneers and the Komsomol (Communist Youth League). The Pioneer organisation (age nine to fourteen) is sometimes compared with the Boy Scout movement in this country with its emphasis on learning to be self-reliant and performing good deeds in the community. The Pioneer code, however, promotes political consciousness as well as a sense of collective responsibility and advocates loyalty to the Motherland, the Party and communism. Atheist instruction is an integral part of this pattern of education. This presents a crisis of conscience for children whose parents are believers and who are taught Christianity at home and a completely different set of values at school.

Atheist propaganda is included in the subject matter of all classes beginning with the fifth year (age eleven). In older forms, atheist instruction is more systematic and in some cases students in their final year at school are required to write essays giving their views on atheism and religion. In universities and other institutes of higher education courses on the fundamentals of scientific atheism are mandatory. Students not only study atheism, but are also expected to participate in atheist work. With help from experienced atheist teachers they lead discussions on atheism, celebrate special atheist days or weeks and help produce atheist displays. As I mentioned before, very few young people who are known to be active Christians will be permitted to study at university or enter any field of higher education. Those who do enter the professions get there despite the system. It is at school-leaving age that the question of ideological indoctrination becomes critical. If students do not apply to join the Komsomol in their final year at school, they will be asked to do so. The majority comply, but few do so out of ideological convictions. Most join more or less because they have to, either as a result of pressure from teachers or parents, or because not to do so would jeopardise their chance of getting into university. Incidentally, Valeri himself was expelled from the Komsomol as a teenager for bad behaviour.

Soviet newspaper articles indicate that the authorities are worried by the apparent loss of idealism and ideological commitment among the young. Hence the repeated urging for improved ideological education on the one hand, and an obsession with statistics on the other. The Soviet daily *Molodezh Moldavii* (Youth of Moldavia) of 4th September, 1984 gives the full text of a lecture entitled 'Improving the role of Komsomol organisations in the communist education of young people', given by the first secretary of the Central Committee of the Lenin Communist Union of Youth, I. Buzhenitsy, at its eleventh plenum. He said:

At the present time, the problem of further improving the standard of atheist education among young people is especially critical.

Every year more than sixty thousand young men and

women fill up the ranks of the republic's Komsomol organisation. The authority and vitality of our (Komsomol) union depends to a large extent upon the willingness of these members to be in the front ranks of the young builders of communism.

About 23,000 young communists honourably carry out their Party commission – to work for the Komsomol. However, Mr Buzhenitsy also criticises some Komsomol organisations where there is 'a very low level of work'. Perhaps the lack of enthusiasm on the part of some young people is partly due to obligatory Komsomol assignments and 'subbotniki' (voluntary working Saturdays) when brigades of young Komsomol members are sent out to perform tasks purported to be socially useful.

When I was studying in Leningrad our Russian room-mates tried to persuade us to join in a 'subbotnik' and help weed the flower beds in a local park. The response was not enthusiastic. The newspaper reporters who deal with this vexed subject do, however, try to give praise where praise is due. They laud the efforts of local Komsomol organisations which zealously run courses of lectures on Marxism-Leninism – even if no one attends them. What, in the Party's view, is the central aim of ideological education? I quote from an article published in *Sovetskaya Moldaviya* (Soviet Moldavia) on 29th August, 1984, entitled 'The formation of a new human being':

> From childhood it is necessary to train a person to think that his social status and material well-being depend primarily on his personal contribution as a member of the socialist work force. He must be taught that an honest, conscientious attitude to his responsibilities as a worker is the basis of socialist society. . . . The efforts of the family, school, the labour collective and the whole of our society should be directed towards this end. . . . This is significant, not only for economic reasons, but for moral reasons, because honest labour is not just a source of material prosperity for the individual, but it

is also a constant source of learning, through which a person develops his creative abilities, strengthens his will and affirms himself as a citizen of the Soviet Union and an active builder of communism.

The formation of a new person is a process which is constantly renewed and which involves many different agencies. But the one factor which is constant, which has never changed and will never do so, is the formation of a scientific, Marxist-Leninist world view – this is the basis of communist education for everyone.

Clearly no concession to religious feelings and convictions is possible within this framework of ideological education. Even though the Soviet education system replaces moral and social values which are based on Christianity with a theoretical socialist morality and a 'Marxist-Leninist world view', this does not prepare people for the reality of living in a totalitarian society. There is no evidence that 'the new socialist man', who lives for the good of the collective and not for himself, has emerged. On the contrary, Soviet people have all the negative as well as positive traits of human nature which one encounters in human beings the world over. They have not been transformed by their socialist system, which is characterised not by 'honest labour' and a 'conscientious attitude to one's responsibilities' – these qualities are rare indeed, except among Christians – but by corruption and illegal private enterprise and a singularly callous disregard for the sanctity of human life.

Valeri's awareness of this anomaly between what he had been taught as a youth and what he saw practised in society was heightened by his experience of army life. This is how he described it:

The following words, found in the Old Testament, were not written in vain: 'I was determined to learn the difference between knowledge and foolishness, wisdom and madness, but I found out that I might as well be chasing the wind' (Ecclesiastes 1.17). After I joined up

25

I despaired of life itself. My circumstances in the army made me think along lines which should be alien to human beings. These were my thoughts – betray your language as best you can, spit on your conscience, on the spirit of comradeship. If someone says to you that something is black and you know it's white, better say it's black and everything will be all right. In other words, be a pawn, don't reason or think things over. There was only one thing of which I was certain – that it would be better to take my own life than to distort my very soul. Although my powers of resistance had already begun to weaken, in my inmost being I believed that there must somewhere be justice and that genuine love must exist. But I didn't know how or where to find these treasures.

What were the conditions for conscripts in the Soviet army which made life so difficult to bear? A book by Victor Suvorov entitled *Inside the Soviet Army* (Hamish Hamilton, 1982) gives us some insight into a Soviet soldier's life. Suvorov is a pseudonym for a man who is just a year or two younger than Valeri and who was an officer in the Soviet army in the post-Khrushchev era. He experienced first-hand the Soviet invasion of Czechoslovakia in 1968. He now lives in the West. I have summarised some of the information from a chapter in the book entitled 'The Soldier's Lot'.

As soon as a young man reaches the age of seventeen he has to appear before a medical board and, if fit, is then listed on the register of those liable for military service. His name remains on the list until the age of fifty and during that time he may be called up without notice if either partial or full mobilisation is announced. When he reaches the age of eighteen he is called up for two years' service (three years if it is in the Navy). There are two intakes of approximately one million young men every year.

The new conscripts are escorted by armed soldiers and

officers to the divisions to which they have been allocated.
Suvorov describes them vividly:

> A new column of recruits is not a sight for anyone with
> weak nerves. Traditionally, anyone joining the army
> dresses in such rags that you wonder where on earth he
> found them. For recruits know that any more or less
> usable article – socks which are not in tatters, for
> instance – will immediately be seized from them by the
> soldiers escorting the column. So they dress in the sort
> of rags which should be thrown on a bonfire – a mech-
> anic's boiler suit, soiled with grease, a painter's working
> clothes daubed with paint of all colours, even a sewage-
> collector's overalls. Many of them will have black eyes,
> acquired in farewell fights with their local enemies. All
> are unshaven, uncombed, shaggy, dirty – and drunk,
> into the bargain. Anyone who has seen for himself what
> a column of these new recruits looks like will under-
> stand why there are no volunteers in the Soviet Army,
> why there never could be and why there is no need for
> them. The whole system is too inflexible, too regulated,
> and too tightly controlled to concern itself with any
> individual's opinions or wishes. Everyone is simply
> grabbed, indiscriminately, as soon as he reaches
> eighteen, and that's that.

Having arrived at their division the new recruits are
issued with uniforms and they begin army life. Long
before this, each individual recruit has been graded and
placed in a certain category, but he is totally unaware that
this process has taken place:

> It does not occur to any of them that each of them has
> already been assessed, taking into account his political
> reliability, his family's criminal record (or absence of
> one), participation (or failure to participate) in commu-
> nist mass meetings, his height and his physical and
> mental development. All these factors have been taken
> into account in grading him as Category 0, 1, 2 and so

forth and then allocating him to a sub-category of one of these groups. . . . They have no idea that they are in this particular category or that files exist on them which have long ago been checked and passed by the KGB.

The first month in a soldier's life is a very tough one during which he is subjected to a rigorous disciplinary programme.

They are chased out of bed twenty or thirty times every night, under pressure to cut seconds off the time it takes them to dress; their days are taken up with training exercises which may last for sixteen hours at a stretch. They study their weapons, they are taught military regulations, they learn the significance of the different stars and insignia on their officers' epaulettes. At the end of the month they fire their own weapons for the first time and then they are paraded to swear the oath of allegiance, knowing that any infringement of this will be heavily punished, even, perhaps, with the death-sentence.

It is at this point that a crisis of conscience occurs for Christian soldiers. Many Christians who are pacifist have refused to swear the oath of allegiance and are sentenced to three years' labour camp as a punishment.

Having survived this first month the recruits are considered to be real soldiers and are distributed among the companies and batteries. The Soviet Army, as every army, has an immovable hierarchical structure. The new recruits become the company's dogs-bodies and they have no choice but to accept their lowly status.

A group of short-haired recruits nervously enters an enormous barrack room, in which two, three or even five hundred soldiers live. They quickly come to realise that they have entered a class-dominated society. Communist theory has no place here. The sergeants split the young soldiers up by platoons, detachments and teams. At first everything goes normally – here is your bed, this is your bedside locker in which you can keep your washing-kit, your four manuals, brushes and your handbook of scientific communism and nothing else. Understand? Yes, sergeant. . . .

But at night the barrack-room comes alive. The recruits need to understand that it contains four classes – the soldiers who will be leaving the army in six months, those who go after a year, a third class who have eighteen months still to serve and, lastly, they themselves, who have a full two years to go. The higher castes guard their privileges jealously. The lower castes must acknowledge their seniors as their elders and betters; the seniors refer to inferiors as 'scum'. Those who still have eighteen months to serve are the superiors of the new recruits, but scum, naturally, to those who have only a year to go. . . .

The lowest class have no rights whatsoever. They clean the shoes and make the beds of their seniors, clean their weapons for them, hand over their meat and sugar rations, sometimes even their bread to them. The soldiers who are soon to be released appropriate the recruits' new uniforms, leaving them with their own worn-out ones. . . .

Six months pass and a new consignment of scum joins your sub-unit. Now those who suffered yesterday have a chance to vent their rage on someone. All the humiliations and insults which they have suffered for six months can now be heaped on the newcomers. Meanwhile those who still insult and beat them up continue to be regarded as scum by their own superiors.

These are the circumstances in which a soldier begins to master the rudiments of the science of war.

Given these tough conditions it is understandable that for most of these men life as a conscript is a matter of making the best of a hopeless situation. The only thing which keeps them going is thinking about demobilisation.

'Roll on my demob!' 'I wish you all a speedy demob – make sure you deserve it!' 'They've taken everything else away, but they can't take my demob!' 'Demobilisation is as inevitable as the collapse of capitalism.' These are sentences you will see scribbled on the wall of any soldiers' lavatory. They are cleaned off every day but they are soon back again, in paint which is still wet.

Demobilisation comes after two years' service. It is the day-dream of every soldier and NCO. From the moment a recruit joins the army, he begins to cross off the days to his demob. He lists the days left on the inside of his belt or ticks them off on a board, a wall or on the side of his tank's engine compartment. In any military camp, on the backs of the portraits of Marx, Lenin, Brezhnev, Andropov and Ustinov you will find scores of inscriptions such as '103 Sundays left to my demob', accompanied by the appropriate number of marks, carefully ticked off one by one in ink or pencil.

Suvorov's account of army life helps us, to some extent, to understand why Valeri, as a raw recruit, was filled with such despair, even to the point of contemplating suicide.

As he had no inner resources to help him to cope he, along with many others, resorted to a favourite Russian pastime – drinking himself into oblivion. His addiction to alcohol became so serious that it was several years before he was able to regain sufficient control of himself to break the drinking habit. Clearly as a result of his own bitter experience, later in life when he began his evangelistic work in Leningrad he showed particular compassion for young people with drink problems.

Faced with the dilemma of where to look for true values in his life, Valeri did not simply turn to the vodka bottle, but began to ask serious questions about Christianity and the existence of God. This is how he describes the process: 'What was it then that happened in my life that made me decide to become a Christian? What led me to a knowledge of the truth? It was simply this – a desire for justice led me to a knowledge of God.'

Valeri describes how he questioned various people about belief in God.

In the army I met one highly-educated man. I thought of him as someone of great intelligence with a real grip on life. But he was domineering and I knew he would not hesitate to ride roughshod over people, even his friends, in order to advance his own career. Because of this I did not entirely trust him, but all the same I decided to find out his opinion about God. Without hesitation he said: 'There is no God. It's all a question of spiritism and hypnosis.' Then I met another man, also well-educated. He was a good man, sincere and modest. I asked him about God. He thought for a while and then said: 'In my opinion there is no God, but all the same there *is* something or other.' So I was given different views about God. The self-confident one said categorically, 'There is no God.' The modest one said that some superior force exists and my aunt, whom I trusted implicitly, declared with total conviction, 'God exists'.

By the time he had reached the final year of army service in 1966 Valeri had earned himself a thoroughly bad reputation for drunkenness and slovenly behaviour. As a result, he was frequently called up before a military tribunal and punished. Following one of his bouts of wild behaviour in Riga, Valeri was locked up in a cell in the guardroom prior to appearing before a tribunal. By this time all Valeri could think of was returning to Leningrad in the hope that civilian life would offer him something better. This was a crucial time because it was shortly before he was due to be demobilised. If the tribunal came down on him severely he might have to serve longer as a punishment. So it was at that particular time that he began to search for God:

From the window of the cell, through the bars, I could see the cross of a church. I was serving in Riga at that time – a town where there are many churches. I was alone in the cell, which was unusual, and this enabled me to do some serious thinking. When I noticed the cross of the church through the bars of the window I remembered what my aunt had said: 'Examine the facts, put them to the test.' This was my first step towards God. If he really existed he would have to help me. There was no question of being hypocritical. I could not bear hypocrisy – my yes was yes and my no was no. Praise God! He helped me. Immediately I went before the tribunal I was cleared.

Valeri was one of the last in his unit to be demobilised and he arrived back in Leningrad in January 1967. He went straight to his aunt. Having proved for himself the existence of God, he would not leave his aunt in peace until she had told him all she knew about God. Valeri described the 'second step' in the following way:

I asked my aunt Tamara how she felt the presence of the Holy Spirit. How do you know you're God's child? My aunt was well aware of my unruly lifestyle and she cautioned me. 'You're trying to go ahead too fast – it's too soon for you.' But in my heart I had firmly resolved to know the presence of the Holy Spirit. I wanted to have God in my heart so that I, too, could be called a child of God. With great persistence I repeated my question. 'Aunt Tamara, tell me what I have to do.' Finally she relented. 'You have to give yourself utterly and completely to God and be at his disposal.'

Later that day Valeri found an opportunity to pray.

With complete confidence that God would now accept me, I said, 'Lord, from this moment I want to belong to you and you alone' (March 1967). I got up from my knees. There were no miracles, no earth tremors, none of the things other people sometimes experience. But I had a tremendous feeling of relief that at last I had taken this step and given myself and all I possessed to God. At that time, the thing that meant most to me was a girl-friend I had had in the army. I had already made up my mind to marry her. But I felt God saying that this was not his will and I thought to myself, Lord, you know better than I do, I will trust you, I put myself in your hands.

Valeri describes the joy and exultation he felt in those first few weeks and the certain knowledge he had that God had made him his son. But he had had no spiritual experience or teaching and very soon he was confronted with the harsh reality of trying to deal with all that was wrong in his life in order to live out his new Christian ideals. He tried to give up smoking and drinking and to forsake all his bad habits, believing that he could somehow summon up the will himself to renounce his former life-style. The result was a rapid decline which Valeri described very vividly.

God had to show me that 'I' was really nothing. I simply fell away. I was defeated. I began to drink heavily again. My aunt's neighbours started to point the finger at her. 'Where is your God?' Poor Aunt Tamara. All she could do was to reply that everything was in the hands of God. One day I got very drunk and when the neighbours found out they locked me in our flat and telephoned my aunt at work. At that time she was working as a midwife and she came home immediately still wearing her surgical gown smeared with blood. By the time she arrived I was in a daze. I had quietened down and was nearly asleep. She got down on her knees and with tears in her eyes said, 'Lord, take this corpse and make a human being out of it'. Because I knew I was not living as I should and had let my aunt down I was thoroughly ashamed of myself. I decided to leave Leningrad and go on a topographical expedition as a driver for the whole summer season.

The next phase of Valeri's life led him thousands of miles away from home to the town of Urai in the Tyumen region of Western Siberia. Western Siberia consists mainly of the Siberian Depression or Lowland, one of the world's largest areas of unbroken flat land. It extends across the country from the foothills of the Urals to the east Siberian highlands and is 1,200 miles from north to south and 900 miles wide at the boundary with Kazakhstan. It was here in the mid-1950s that Soviet geologists discovered vast reserves of oil and natural gas. Huge capital investments were made in the region in the early sixties and the oil and gas reserves are recognised as of the greatest importance to the Soviet Union, and also as a source of supply for East European countries and as earners of hard currency from customers in Western Europe. Oil and gas production figures have risen spectacularly since the early sixties.

Compared with deposits in more moderate climates, the cost of developing natural gas and oil in the Tyumen region is very high because of the harsh natural conditions. The largest gas wells lie well within the Arctic Circle and the permafrost zone, where the cost of geological research, labour and transport is high. The town of Urai where Valeri eventually found himself is situated in the foothills of the Ural mountains and is located in one of the main oil-bearing areas in Western Siberia.

From the earliest days of exploration a corps of skilled and unskilled workers has been needed, but maintaining this work force has been a major problem for the government. Conditions are so hard that there is a rapid turnover of workers. Very high wages will not, in themselves, guarantee that people will stay indefinitely in a harsh climate where social and domestic amenities are far from ideal. Over a seven-year period from 1963 one Soviet expert estimated that 80 per cent of incoming migrants left the Tyumen region, primarily because of the living conditions.

Valeri gives no indication of what he was actually doing when he arrived in Urai, but he soon made his presence felt.

Not long after I had arrived in Urai I turned up at a concert, or rather a dance. I sang a few numbers and was invited to stay and eventually they asked me to become the leader of the group.

And so Valeri became involved in a small local group which gave regular concerts. This was the time when Western rock music was having an unprecedented impact on the lives of Soviet young people. Beatlemania had engulfed Moscow and Leningrad, spread to the provinces and even reached Western Siberia in the mid-1960s. Valeri, with his repertoire of Rolling Stones and Beatles songs – he even looked a bit like a Beatle – became an immediate success. At that time he was a completely secular musician, but his awareness of the tangible impact of pop and rock music on his young audiences must have influenced him later when he was thinking about forming a Christian band.

In order to appreciate Valeri's role, both as a secular musician and later as a specifically Christian composer, one has to understand something about the development in the Soviet Union since the beginning of the twentieth century of a popular culture in which music has played a very significant role. (For information on this subject I have drawn extensively on S. Frederick Starr's *Red & Hot: The Fate of Jazz in the Soviet Union* (Oxford University Press, 1983).)

Popular American culture at the turn of the century manifested itself in many diverse forms, but the form which had perhaps the greatest impact on social life and every sphere of the arts was jazz. Playing jazz represented a form of liberation, a style of music where the individual musician could do just as he liked and the outcome was music that was exciting and unlike anything that had been heard before.

Starr describes how ragtime music, to a large extent the precursor of jazz, was pioneered in the USA in the early 1890s, had enormous impact in England and Western Europe and became popular in pre-revolutionary Russia in 1910. Just as important as the new music were the new dance forms that went with it, in particular the cakewalk. This was a dance originally performed by urbanised American blacks as a parody of the formal ballroom dances of the 1880s. On the eve of the Revolution in 1917, St Petersburg society was familiarising itself with the one-step, the Boston and the fox-trot performed to the accompaniment of American dance tunes.

It was not until a few years later, however, that jazz really took root in the Soviet Union. Between 1918 and 1920 the country was engulfed in a civil war and during the early years of the revolution it was isolated from the West.

International links which had earlier brought the latest recordings of popular music to Russia had been severed. The new, non-convertible currency made it impossible for the nationalised publishing industry to purchase Western scores of popular music even if it had wanted to. As a result, the only Western popular tunes that were issued were several years out of date. This isolation also affected the record industry in Russia at a time when, in 1922, 110 million records were produced in the US and Western Europe alone and much of that music was jazz.

However, these seemingly insurmountable barriers were overcome largely by the efforts of a certain Valentin Parnakh, a Russian who had emigrated before the First World War and discovered jazz while living in Paris. He returned to Moscow in 1922 and launched the first ever Russian jazz band.

From the early 1920s to the present day jazz has thrived in the Soviet Union and has won acclaim among the highest levels of leadership. It has, in turn, been denounced by the government as decadent and bourgeois and acclaimed as a great proletarian art form. The various shifts in government policy have given rise to some curious anomalies, such as the presence of Soviet jazz bands at the front during the Second World War raising the morale of the Soviet troops; the virtual disappearance of the saxophone during the last few years of Stalin's oppressive reign; the enormously successful performances given by a famous jazz band in the Gulag Archipelago comprising jazz musicians who were victims of Stalin's purges and the extraordinary story of the rise and survival of jazz in Estonia, where the first ever Soviet jazz festival took place in May 1948, six years before the inauguration of the Newport Jazz Festival in the USA.

During the fifties and early sixties there emerged a new generation of alienated urban Russian youth who were genuinely discontented with public life, cynical and apolitical and who attempted to create their own subculture. An important part of that subculture was jazz, not least because in the years after Stalin's death jazz was being rigorously denounced by Stalinists who were still in office. Starr writes:

> Jazz with its emphasis on individuality and personal expression became the *lingua franca* of dissident Soviet youth.

In 1955 the programme 'Music USA', designed specifically for Soviet youth, was first broadcast to the Soviet Union by the radio station, Voice of America. These broadcasts of popular music and jazz provided a mass of new material for young aspiring Soviet musicians. Such programmes devoted to jazz, but more significantly to rock music, are still broadcast and are enormously popular among Soviet youth today.

The so-called festival movement which began in Tallinn and gathered momentum in the early 1960s until jazz festivals were being held in Moscow, Leningrad and a number of other Soviet cities, reached its peak during the May festival held in Tallinn in 1967. However, domestic and international events which occurred at the same time, notably the rise of political dissent within the Soviet Union and the flowering of the 'Prague Spring' which resulted in the invasion by Soviet troops of Czechoslovakia in 1968, led to a curtailment of many of the advances made by Soviet jazz musicians. Many subsequently emigrated from the Soviet Union. For those that remained, a new problem confronted them which was by no means confined to jazz musicians in the Soviet Union – the rise of rock music.

Starr comments:

> Within fifteen years the modern jazz revolution of the late fifties had been swept aside by the music of the Beatles and the Rolling Stones, Stevie Wonder and the Shadows.

Would-be rock musicians faced the same problems in obtaining instruments as had the jazz musicians of the 1920s. Electric guitars, not manufactured in the Soviet Union but obtainable from Poland and East Germany, were brought into the country mainly by exchange students and sold on the black market at vastly inflated prices. Some guitarists built their own guitars and amplifiers and tens of thousands of instruments were produced 'privately' and distributed through the black market. Some of the instruments were of such poor quality that they were virtually useless, but some were the work of real craftsmen.

Starr describes one black-market guitar maker from Odessa who copied Fender and Marshall instruments so well, even adding adaptations, that foreign musicians visiting Odessa on cruise ships would exchange the genuine articles for his forgeries.

Rock music was officially banned, but when the Beatles craze overtook the Soviet Union in the mid-sixties attempts to reinforce the ban only led to the flourishing of an underground rock culture. Dozens of new rock bands emerged and in the late sixties they were all strongly influenced by British bands. Cliff Richard's Shadows were as popular as the Beatles. Many of the new Soviet bands sang their lyrics in English as a deliberate affront to the older generation because the study of foreign languages was a privilege enjoyed mainly by the young.

Together with this new rebellious music went long hair, miniskirts and all the other trappings of the rock subculture, as well as heavy drinking and the use of soft drugs. Once this trend started, no official attempts to reverse it could succeed. Starr observes:

> The cultivation of purposeful deviance and outright rebellion among Soviet youth reached a new high with the appearance in the late seventies of aggressively anti-social punk and heavy metal bands. Such groups deliberately assaulted respectable society with garish costumes, ferocious volume and obscene lyrics.

Many of the more offensive bands were stamped out by local authorities, but despite attempts to contain this new social disease and subject it to censorship many rock bands continued to flourish. Starr remarks:

> In 1969 it was estimated that there was not a high school, institute or factory in Moscow without at least one rock band, bringing the total to several thousand and meaning that several thousand private and independent producers were operating in the field of popular culture.

In 1969 the KGB made a serious attempt to exert official control over rock music in Moscow. The Komsomol's 'Melody' café, established in the early 1960s as a jazz café and later renamed the Melody and Rhythm café, set up a Beat Club offering attractive incentives to registered members. Many of Moscow's best rock musicians were enticed on to the board of the Beat Club which then announced that it would hold open auditions for membership. Tempted by the promise of concerts and imported instruments and amplifiers people queued to register, but this involved filling out a detailed questionnaire touching on every aspect of the applicants' biography. Once the registration was complete, the activities of the Beat Club dwindled, but the KGB had complete files on hundreds of the best rock musicians in the Moscow region.

Some musicians managed to adapt their style and repertoire sufficiently in order to become officially acceptable, but it was then difficult for them to retain the spontaneity they had possessed earlier, so they risked losing some of their popularity. Some bands such as the 'Happy Guys' (Veselye Rebyata), formed in 1968 to promote an image of healthy Soviet youth to young audiences, set out deliberately to conform to the whims of the State concert agencies who paid their salaries, in order to guarantee their livelihood.

During the era of détente in the seventies a number of American and European rock bands were permitted to tour the Soviet Union and this further hindered the government's attempts to control rock music. The Soviet authorities simply have to admit that, despite all their efforts, they have utterly failed to provide an acceptable alternative to Western popular culture. It is hard to imagine how, given the ease of modern communications, the influence of this alien culture can be kept at bay.

In recent years, particularly under the rule of Mr Chernenko, strongly-worded attacks have been launched more consistently in the Soviet press against the harmful influence of rock. There have even been reports by doctors testifying to the 'tremendously harmful psychic effect' of rock music leading to hysteria and convulsions. Such articles are invariably commented upon with great glee by Western correspondents writing about the Soviet Union. In the month of August 1984 alone there were three major articles in different newspapers devoted to various aspects of youth subculture. The headlines speak for themselves: 'Why the Kremlin is taking punk fashion seriously: Sergei's safety pins needle Moscow' (*The Times*, 28th August); 'Soviet Call to control teenagers' (the *Daily Telegraph*, 30th August); 'T-shirts in Russia become site of battle for influence' (*International Herald Tribune*, 25th August). More recently in an article entitled 'Soviet pop stars clean up their act' (the *Observer*, 7th April, 1985), Mark Frankland described how rock groups, both professional and amateur, as well as discothèques, had to submit to a series of tests. The judges, consisting of bureaucrats from the Ministry of Culture, trade union and party youth officials, representatives of the local authorities and some ordinary citizens have deemed that many of the groups are failures. Lists of banned Soviet and foreign groups have been compiled for the benefit of discos and youth clubs. At the time of writing (May 1985) there has been a spate of articles in the Western press about Mr Gorbachov's strict measures to deal with the alarming problem of alcoholism in the Soviet Union. It seems likely that he may also attempt to 'disinfect' the milieu which often gives rise to drunkenness among young people, the underworld of rock culture, and that would mean a further crack-down on rock music.

However, there are some signs that the authorities recognise that alongside banning and tighter controls, there will have to be a certain amount of compromise.

While constantly denouncing the harmful effects of ideologically unacceptable Western music which, they claim, is inspired by the CIA, there have also been some attempts to start a debate among young people on this issue. An interesting article appeared in *Molodezh Moldavii* (Youth of Moldavia) in November 1984 by Vitali Kiselev who is described as the 'leading DJ' at the Erma electrical factory. He begins by criticising the level of expertise demonstrated by the average Soviet DJ which, he claims, to a large extent determines the success of a disco. He then gives his own view on the necessary qualifications for a good DJ:

Unfortunately, in many of our discos the DJs are just not up to the job and what should be one of the most interesting types of leisure activity for young people is transformed into a boring evening of dance.... Who is in charge of these discos? In nine cases out of ten people who have some technical education. Of course, DJs must have some technical knowhow, but in my opinion what is much more important is that they should have had some musical education. Music is one of the most powerful means of education, of forming a world view.

Konstantin Chaikovsky once said, 'Music is a powerful weapon which can arouse people – it's like a medicine. It can poison and it can heal.' Just as medicine should be in the hands of specialists, so too, should music.

Frequently DJs know absolutely nothing about a particular band apart from the name. They don't know what constitutes the features of a certain style or musical trend. They cannot therefore guide their public.

The ideal DJ, in my opinion, should first of all be a personality in his own right. He should also be a sensitive, intelligent and thoughtful person, a good communicator with good manners who can speak well and attract people's attention.

While there is much to be said in support of an attempt to raise the 'cultural level' of some young people, both East and West, and no doubt many parents would have great sympathy with this young man's views, to the majority of Soviet young people who simply want to break free from all constraints and have a good time he probably sounds unbearably priggish.

Kiselev mentions the positive role of the local Komsomol organisation in making the Erma disco a success. However, he also admits that many DJs face problems which make their task very difficult and which are sometimes impossible to overcome. The main problems he lists are those of finding an adequate location for a disco and obtaining the necessary equipment and records. He also complains that young people are rarely permitted to travel beyond their city boundaries and cannot therefore attend discos in other towns or republics and pick up new ideas to improve their own discos. The fact that he admits that conditions are not ideal and encourages an exchange of correspondence on the subject is significant.

However, if we return now to Urai in 1967, it is not difficult to understand, given his musical talents, why Valeri had such enormous success playing in clubs and restaurants with other local musicians.

But at the same time Valeri was still struggling as a Christian. Reflecting on that period in his life, he identified one of the main problems as a lingering regret about the girl-friend he had left behind. He felt that in this respect God had given him a very difficult test. He was still trying to live the Christian life in his own strength and had not learned to offer every situation to God and to trust Him. Once again God had to show Valeri that he could never hope to survive as a Christian while relying on his own strength. Valeri described another vivid incident which finally brought him to his senses:

There were times when God tested me and I simply couldn't endure it. God wanted to blot out the 'I' in my life and make me understand that I couldn't achieve anything by myself and that God alone could transform me into a real Christian. So how did I manage to give up drinking? It had been going on unbroken for about a year and a half. I shall never forget the time when I had no money to buy a drink or even anything to eat. My friend and I decided to go and get a bite in a snack bar. All I could think of was how to get hold of one rouble to get something to eat. I had already begun to think to myself – OK Valeri, today you'll give up drinking. You'll have something to eat and in the evening you'll sober up. You'll feel quite normal and then you'll pray to God. For a long time I had had a desire to pray about my drink problem and to ask God to stop me. But I always thought in terms of *my* taking the initiative, of it being my decision. Yes, of course a time would come when I would get down on my knees, but in the meantime the devil would not give in.

When we arrived at the snack bar we looked around and there was a bottle of vodka standing on a table.

Of course, we drank it.

Some time later I had a dream. I dreamt of my uncle, my former guardian. He had passed on, but before his death he had become a Christian. I was on my way to see him in an unfamiliar room. I walked into the middle of the room, but I was afraid to go right up to him because I felt guilty. My uncle looked at me severely and said: 'You should at least have wiped your feet.' I looked down and saw that my legs were covered with mud right up to my knees. Then I woke up. I got down on my knees and in tears I repented and said, 'Lord, I am perishing, save me.'

Valeri does not give his own interpretation of the dream, but to me it is very simple. In his dream a third of his body was covered with mud, and in his life as a Christian there was still much that was dishonouring to God. There were sins clinging to him which he had not managed to shake off. His subsequent act of repentance came from the heart and very soon afterwards he was to experience a great blessing.

One day Valeri walked into the post office in Urai to make a long-distance telephone call to Leningrad. He was immediately struck by the telephone operator, a beautiful girl in her teens with red hair and green eyes. This was his first meeting with Tanya who was eventually to become his wife. They got to know each other over a period of about eight months and it was then that Valeri decided that this was the girl he wanted to marry. The wedding took place on 27th December, 1968, when Tanya was only eighteen. Tanya was not a Christian at that time and Valeri's ideas about Christianity were entirely new to her; she even found them rather amusing.

Tanya was born in 1950 in Volgograd and was one of a large family with five children. Initially all Tanya's family warmed to Valeri and liked him for his easy-going nature and positive character. However, later on when he became more committed and active as a Christian they kept their distance from him. Tanya's mother, in particular, turned against Valeri and tried to persuade Tanya to leave him. Tanya gave birth to their first child, Zhanna, in October 1969 and because of his newfound happiness in family life and fatherhood, Valeri gradually managed to overcome his drink problem. However, there were still difficulties in his Christian life because there was no opportunity to learn about the Christian faith.

When drawing up the plans for new towns in these vast undeveloped regions, the Soviet planners made no provision for churches and today there are very few churches in any of the new cities. According to Walter Sawatsky, an expert on the history of evangelicals in the Soviet Union, there are groups of Reform Baptists – Baptists who meet secretly and whose churches are not officially registered by the state – scattered throughout Western Siberia, and there are large numbers of unregistered Pentecostals. But the official Baptist organisation, the All Union Council of Evangelical Christians and Baptists (AUCECB) is poorly represented in this region. In 1974 one of the senior presbyters belonging to the AUCECB, a man named Raevsky, received one single assistant to help him to administer a territory which covered over 20 million square kilometres. At the same time the senior presbyter for Western Siberia, Konstantin Borodinov, tried to visit all the registered churches throughout this vast region. There was not only a problem of distance, but for years the senior presbyter could not automatically travel where he wished.

In recent years there has been some improvement with regard to AUCECB churches in Western Siberia. New churches have been registered in the Omsk and Tomsk regions, adjacent to the Tyumen region, and a senior presbyter has been appointed for the Omsk region.

There may have been small, isolated groups of Christians meeting for worship within travelling distance of Urai, but if there were, Valeri did not appear to know about them. He became homesick for Leningrad. Not only was he tired of living in that region for the usual geographical reasons, but also he had a tremendous longing to hear the word of God preached and to be near his Aunt Tamara who would be able to give him guidance in his Christian life. He began to pray for direction. In March 1971 the Barinov family moved to Leningrad, to the communal flat at Trinity Fields where Valeri had been born. Valeri started a job as a driver attached to a car depot. He began to attend the registered Baptist Church at Poklonnaya Gora in the north east of the city. He was baptised in September of the same year and so became a full member of the church. This marked the beginning of a period when Valeri was to grow tremendously in wisdom and stature as a Christian and to start responding to God's call to all his disciples: 'Go and preach the Gospel to all nations.'

3: Decades of persecution

I have indicated that the odds are very much against young people turning to the Christian faith in the Soviet Union and yet there is abundant evidence that in that vast country today young people are looking in increasing numbers to churches of all denominations for spiritual guidance. What are the churches able to offer? What freedom do they have to spread the Christian faith and what makes them attractive to genuine 'seekers'? These are all questions which will be answered, at least in part, as the story of Valeri's own calling to preach the gospel unfolds. However, in order to understand the attitudes of the older generation we must know something about the post-Revolutionary history of the Church there. Because Valeri himself is an Evangelical Christian, I shall confine what I have to say to the Evangelicals, except where other comparisons are useful.

Valeri, of course, knew very little about the history of Evangelicals in his country, or the structure of the Baptist Church, except what he had heard from his Aunt Tamara. But he was eager to learn and gained a great deal of knowledge by talking to believers of his aunt's generation – those who had been born around the time of the Revolution.

In order to reconstruct some of the fascinating and tragic history of Soviet Evangelicals I would like to recount an imaginary conversation between myself and a close friend and contemporary of Valeri's Aunt Tamara, Maria Petrovna, which might have taken place on my last visit to the Soviet Union in 1982. The conversation as such never took place, but here and there I heard snatches of it from different people and the basic facts as told by Maria Petrovna are historically accurate. But before our conversation begins, there are a few general observations to be made.

The history of Christianity in the Soviet Union since 1917 is one of repeated waves of revival and persecution, but for some branches of the Christian faith persecution began in the mid-nineteenth century, long before the Revolution. At that time religious life in Russia was dominated by the partnership between the Tsar and the Russian Orthodox Church. At various times throughout that century the Russian Orthodox hierarchy reacted strongly against the reformist tendencies of Russian Evangelicals who had been much influenced by the Protestant Pietist movement in other parts of Europe. Many Evangelicals were subjected to arrests, fines, imprisonments and long periods in exile in an attempt to dampen and curtail their missionary zeal and stop them gaining converts from the ranks of the Orthodox. Despite these setbacks, the Evangelicals remained undaunted and a measure of relief came with a series of acts of toleration in 1905 when it became possible to leave the Orthodox Church and join the confession of one's choice. The Evangelicals immediately took advantage of this new situation and organised a systematic expansion of their missionary work. However, within a few years the political climate had changed again and additional laws were introduced further restricting their activities. The Revolution of 1917, with its decree separating churches from the State, was therefore a great source of hope for the Evangelicals and the first decade under the new communist system, surprisingly, was one of growth in all branches of evangelical Christianity. At this point Maria Petrovna begins her story, which I interrupt from time to time with my questions.

M.P.   I was a tiny child at the time of the Revolution. We were living in St Petersburg, as it was then, and both my parents were strong believers – we were

Baptists. We always used to have family prayers and Bible readings so I grew up in an atmosphere where God was always at the centre of our thoughts and activities.

The Revolution brought many changes and in some ways life was chaotic, but for the believers it was an exciting time. There was a new decree which made it possible for people to profess whatever belief they chose and not to be penalised for it – at least that's what it was taken to mean. There were many evangelical churches in Leningrad in those days – about six or seven – and the numbers of converts kept increasing. There were two unions, one for the evangelicals and one for the Baptists, and they were even allowed to publish a limited amount of Christian literature. It wasn't so rare to see Bibles and Christian song books, and some Christian books were imported from abroad. So the believers had the basic tools for evangelism.

L.B. But it must have been difficult to provide enough pastors and teachers to look after these new converts. How did the churches manage?

M.P. Well, the Baptist Union started Bible schools in Moscow and Kiev and the Evangelical Christians organised one in Leningrad. I remember my father saying how much he wished he could give up his job with the railway and go and study the Bible full-time. But the Bible schools were mainly for training preachers and he didn't feel that that was his calling. Instead he used to go and listen to as many sermons as he could and make notes on them. There were some very fine preachers at that time.

My father especially admired Ivan Prokhanov, one of the great evangelical leaders, who was a socialist and a great visionary who wanted to build a model city, a kind of Christian commune where everyone would live together in peace and harmony. His ideas seemed to be along the same lines as those put forward by our new Communist leaders – that everyone should be equal and share whatever they possessed for the good of all.

L.B.   But surely, Maria Petrovna, the new communist leaders were completely against religion? Didn't Lenin say that religion and socialism were incompatible and that Marxism was totally hostile to religion?

M.P.   Yes, of course that's true, but in the early days the authorities weren't so worried about the Evangelical Christians. We were so small in numbers compared with the millions of Orthodox believers. The real offensive was against the Russian Orthodox Church. They suffered terribly in those early years, with all the leaders – and many others – being imprisoned and most churches closed. And, of course, to some extent the authorities were being more lenient towards us to play us off against the Orthodox and because Evangelical Christians had suffered a great deal under the Tsars. Perhaps they thought we would ultimately be more willing to co-operate with them in 'building socialism'. But the Evangelicals knew that it wasn't going to be easy for long.

By the end of the 1920s Stalin had organised an all-out attack on religion. A law was passed in April 1929 which took away virtually all our religious rights. A complicated procedure for registering local congregations was introduced and until you obtained your registration, all religious activity was forbidden. For example, a preacher could only work in the immediate area where the members of his congregation were living, so no missionary outreach was possible beyond it. Special meetings for children, youth and women were banned, as well as all charitable work organised through the church. As soon as this law was implemented the life of the church came to a virtual standstill. Ministers were arrested, churches were closed and believers were terrified. Even those who tried to comply with the new procedures often came unstuck, because of the bureaucracy involved and the unwillingness of the authorities to grant registration. On the other hand, those who did manage to register lived with the constant threat that the permission would be revoked on the slightest pretext. Nearly all our leaders disappeared into prison and exile and were never seen again. Twelve Baptist ministers in Leningrad were arrested in 1930 and all our churches except one were confiscated. I was too young at the time to remember any of the ministers clearly, but I had made friends with the daughter of one of them. She was the same age as me and was one of seven children. She never saw her father again. . . .

L.B. What happened next – did the church simply cease to exist?

M.P. There was virtually no organised religious life. It was too dangerous. The believers just used to meet quietly in each others' homes to pray and read the Bible. Then the war broke out and everything changed. Of course, whenever there is a national crisis people turn to God more than at any other time. Well, Stalin didn't turn to God, but he stopped persecuting the Church, at least, for the time being, because he knew that otherwise people would be completely demoralised and wouldn't be able to put anything into the war effort.

There were one or two Evangelical leaders who had actually managed to avoid imprisonment and they became active in patriotic work, especially a man called Mikhail Orlov who later became pastor of our Church in Leningrad and a very prominent church leader. I suspect that he was put under great pressure by the authorities. At one time the Evangelical leaders were absolutely unanimous in their pacifist views, but Orlov must have had a complete change of heart, because after Hitler invaded our country in 1941 he began to organise big rallies and to urge believers to join the Red Army. Well, of course, people did, everyone joined in the war effort – it was our patriotic duty. Then at the end of the war in 1944 our two unions finally merged and we became the All Union Council of Evangelical Christians and Baptists (AUCECB). Many people were unhappy about the new union because they felt that the principles on which it was based had not been worked out properly. At the end of the war the church was no longer under siege, the restrictions had been relaxed and there was some freedom to preach the Gospel again. After the terrible suffering of the war years, people were even more open to hear the word of God and there was a huge revival. We lost 20 million people during the war and in Leningrad alone about one million died during the siege, most of starvation. You don't easily forget suffering like that. This made some people bitter and they turned against all religion, but many more entered the Kingdom of God.

L.B.   What were you doing at the time?

M.P.   Well, I was in my late twenties when the war ended. I had been trained as a nurse and I don't think I could have survived that period without my faith. The hospitals were full of war wounded and we simply didn't have enough trained staff or sufficient medical supplies to care for them. People were dying every day and all I could do was try to offer some comfort by speaking about the Lord Jesus. I had many Christian friends at that time and we all supported each other, meeting as often as we could for prayer. I remember some extraordinary stories that filtered through to our circle in Leningrad about whole villages in far away regions of the country being converted to Christianity. Of course, by that time many travelling evangelists were back on the road. There was no religious literature to speak of, no Bibles or song books, because nothing had been printed for fifteen years or more, so people had to rely on the spoken word and write down what they could whenever a sermon was preached.

L.B. But I still don't understand how the authorities tolerated this revival. Surely they hadn't changed their policy towards religion overnight?

M.P. At that time there were tremendous difficulties in the life of our country. The economy had to be rebuilt from top to bottom after the ravages of the war, so the leaders were more interested in mobilising the work force and putting industry back on its feet than in anything else. But, of course, they still kept a close watch on what was happening in the churches. They wanted loyalty from the top church leaders, and they allowed a journal to be published as a concession.

The state set up two special bodies to deal with liaison between church and state, one for the Orthodox Church and one for all non-Orthodox churches and other religions. Eventually they were merged to form one body, the Council for Religious Affairs (CRA) which, of course, still exists today. It was obvious from the beginning that this was simply a way of interfering and trying to control church life despite all the excuses to the contrary. Even some of our own Baptist leaders have tried to pretend that the CRA is in some way serving our own interests. But, of course, it isn't. How could it be? It's simply an arm of our atheist government. How can atheists be expected to be sympathetic to the needs of believers? The truth of the matter is that there is more or less open warfare between church and state. Anyhow, to get back to the 1940s, it wasn't long before there was a new crackdown on religious life. From 1949 until Stalin died in 1953 there was terrible persecution. Those who suffered most were Christians who had either refused or been unable to register their church with the authorities. The pastors of any of those congregations who dared to preach were immediately arrested. Many of them were given twenty-five-year sentences. So much for separation of church and state! Churches were closed and once again everyone was afraid that organised church life would be wiped out completely.

L.B. So what happened after Stalin died? Were the churches reopened?

M.P. No, not many churches reopened, but things improved for a few years. Many people who had been given long prison sentences under Stalin and had survived the camps were rehabilitated and there were many believers and preachers among them. But it was only a breathing space.

Our next leader, Nikita Khrushchev, was violently opposed to religion. I suppose the communist rulers must have realised by this time that religion was simply not going to die out. They had tried terror but even that didn't work, so as well as the terror they tried a new tactic. It was called ideological education. A new society was formed in 1960 which was supposed to spread scientific and political knowledge. Nowadays it's called the *Znanie*

(Knowledge) society and they are responsible for organising atheist lectures and debates to try and prove that God does not exist. In those days the top political leaders were involved in the debate and they instructed all the regional Party organisations to enforce the laws on religion.

L.B.　Were those the laws passed in 1929?

M.P.　Yes, more or less, except there had been some amendments. For example in 1959 the Criminal Code of the Russian republic was revised and you could be sentenced for up to five years' imprisonment just for organising a Bible study or religious discussion group or teaching religion to children. Of course, this led to thousands of arrests and once again churches everywhere were closed, pulled down, or turned into warehouses or museums. Many of us asked ourselves at that time how much more we would have to endure. But our faith remained the most precious thing. Too much blood had been shed and too many lives sacrificed for us to give up the struggle. In fact in many ways, it was at that particular time that our faith became stronger than ever before. There was a great deal at stake and I don't just mean our personal freedom, family life and security – the integrity of our faith was on trial.

In 1961 the authorities forced some of our Baptist leaders to accept new regulations affecting church life. All the senior presbyters were issued with a 'letter of instructions' which set out how the new regulations were to be applied. It was scandalous. The preachers were told that they mustn't make appeals during services for people to become Christians, children were to be banned from services and pastors were told to reduce the number of baptisms of young people. In other words, we were being told to disobey the commands of Christ – and even to do less than the existing laws permitted. Well, all this led to a terrible split in the church, which persists to this day. Many believers simply refused to submit to these instructions and a so-called Initiative Group was immediately formed which protested strongly to the Moscow Baptist leadership. This group eventually formed an opposition movement led initially by two men called Prokofiev and Kryuchkov soon joined by Georgi Vins.

The movement came to be known as the Initsiativniki or the Reform Baptists. They began to work on a document revising all the regulations which the AUCECB leadership had introduced. They also wrote many appeals to the state leaders, challenging them to uphold our constitution which guarantees freedom of religion.

Before long, these appeals were being passed around from hand to hand; copies were made and this strengthened people's resolve not to give in to the restrictions being imposed on them by the state via the AUCECB. The opposition movement won a good deal of support from ordinary believers and many of them felt great resentment towards their own leaders, judging that they had made a cowardly compromise. Prokofiev was soon arrested and got five years' camp and five years' exile, then they arrested Kryuchkov in 1966. But others took over the leadership of the Reform Baptists. It's been like that virtually ever since. There has never been a time when Baptists outside the AUCECB haven't been badly persecuted.

L.B. But what happened to the Reformers? Did they break away completely from the AUCECB?

M.P. There were some attempts at reconciliation with the official Union – they still go on – but what hope was there for this when all the Reform leaders were in prison? Eventually they set up their own organisation, the Council of Churches of Evangelical Christians and Baptists (CCECB) and I must say, despite the persecution, they've done some wonderful work. In many ways they put us registered Baptists to shame. I don't really feel separate from the Reformers. Our faith is the same and our love for the Lord is the same. They've managed to produce hundreds of thousands of Bibles and other Christian literature on secret printing presses. And they don't just keep it for themselves, they share it with all believers. They have a secret publication called the *Bulletin* which is produced by the wives of men who are in prison for their faith and they regularly send information abroad about the latest situation in their churches. They have a system for providing aid to the prisoners' relatives, so that no one is left destitute, and they even manage to organise secret Sunday schools and summer camps, so that children can hear the gospel. They pay a heavy price, though. There are over 200 of them in prison at the moment.

L.B. You didn't finish telling me what it was like under Krushchev or what happened after he fell from favour. Have things improved since then? What do you think of the AUCECB leadership today?

M.P. Well, Khrushchev did a lot of damage, but as you know, he fell from power in 1964. That was nearly twenty years ago and it's hard to remember all that's happened since. But, of course, the main thing is that Christianity hasn't died out. There are new generations of Christians – like our Valeri, who gives us so much heartache. And now his two girls are believers and so it goes on.

I'm an old woman now. I count myself fortunate. I've never had to suffer physically for my faith in the way others have, in the camps or in exile. But I've seen it happening to others before my very eyes. Like that young girl's father who was dragged off to prison for nothing, never to return or see his family again. Yes, the brutality is still with us today, you've only to open your eyes and unstop your ears and the evidence is in front of you. But the Lord remains our hope and our strength and we simply have to go on trusting in him and there will always be others to continue the struggle.

4: Ministry and rejection

In 1977 I was fortunate to have an opportunity to study Russian for three months at Leningrad University under the auspices of the British Council. I knew very little about the situation of the church in the Soviet Union before I left England, but nothing could have prepared me for the intensely moving experience of meeting Russian Christians and learning about Russian spirituality in an atheist society. A fellow Christian in my group, Diana, who became a close friend, had prepared herself better than I, because she had been very closely in touch with Keston College prior to our departure for the Soviet Union and had with her the addresses of various churches in Leningrad and the names of individual contacts.

On one memorable occasion, not long after we had arrived in Leningrad, we travelled miles outside the city by train and bus to a tiny country village. Leaving the main road, we walked along a dirt track until we came to a group of wooden houses, each with its own fenced garden and huge woodpile. It was hard to estimate how many people had crammed into the house we entered, but they were overflowing into the porch. This was a birthday celebration and such occasions are often used by Russian Christians as a pretext for an evangelistic gathering, which enhanced the joyful family occasion. If, as sometimes happened, the militia came to investigate the meeting, the participants would have a legitimate reason for being present.

People continued to drift in and out throughout the afternoon, but as soon as all the main body of people had gathered, at once the testimonies began. Each person took a turn to recite a poem, sing a song or read a passage from the Bible. Christian literature is virtually unobtainable in the Soviet Union and very few of those present had a Bible or a hymn book. Many believers compile their own 'Bible notebooks'. These are beautifully-produced hand-written compilations of Bible passages. The verses of scripture are jotted down during sermons and arranged according to themes, often with a written testimony by the compiler. And so each person who sang or read explained why the verse or passage or poem was important and what could be learnt from it. As well as a personal insight, they always tried to give a wider application which would be helpful to the whole group. People listened intently, revering every word that was said. These testimonies were interspersed with joyful outbursts of singing affirming the great truths of the Christian faith and times of individual fervent prayer.

The meeting lasted for several hours and during this time a meal was served. But even while people were eating there was no relaxation of their intense concentration on the spiritual matters being discussed. I had never experienced such a gathering before and I felt while I was in the room that nothing else seemed to matter. The harsh reality of the atheist society in which these Christians were living seemed irrelevant, so absorbed were they in sharing their profound spiritual experiences.

This truly was a company of people who were in the world but not of it. There was no hint of bitterness or hatred expressed when some of them shared the hardships they faced, the insults they had suffered and the discrimination they had endured because they were known to be believers.

Going home in the train that evening I was mentally exhausted and felt as if I had stepped into a different world. I was tired not only because I had concentrated on the Russian language for so many hours, but also because of the unbroken intensity with which all the conversations had been conducted. I had a deep admiration and respect for these brothers and sisters, but found it very difficult to relate their experience to my own Christian life which, by comparison, seemed shallow and worldly. As we said goodbye at the end of our journey, the young people urged us to come again the following week to a meeting of Reform Baptists at a house in a neighbouring village. Yes, of course we would come, I thought, but I remember feeling thankful that I would have a good breathing space in between.

The following week we were warmly welcomed at the church service which took place in the home of Vladimir Protsenko. The service had just the same intensity as the 'birthday' meeting, but was much more formal. Afterwards we had the privilege of meeting Aida Skripnikova. Aida had already at that time served two prison sentences. In 1961, on New Year's Eve, as a very new Christian she stood in Nevsky Prospekt, the main shopping street in Leningrad, and distributed postcards on which she had written a Christian poem. It emphasised the need for every single human being to search for and find God while they still had time.

She was arrested and tried by a Comrades' Court, but it was several years before the court carried out its decision to dismiss her from her job as a laboratory assistant and take away her residence permit so that she could no longer live in Leningrad. In the meantime she became involved with the Council of Churches of Evangelical Christians and Baptists (CCECB) and worked for them distributing their publications and passing on information about arrests and trials of believers to foreign visitors.

In 1965 she was again arrested, this time at a prayer meeting held in a forest. She was tried and sentenced to one year in prison. After her release she again encountered many difficulties because of her Christian beliefs and eventually was arrested in April 1968 and sentenced to three years' imprisonment for her work for the CCECB. Her story is told in *Aida of Leningrad* by Michael Bourdeaux and Xenia Howard-Johnston (Gateway Outreach, 1972; out of print). She talked to us briefly about her circumstances. What I remember most vividly is her face which looked older than her thirty-six years – doubtless as a result of the harsh conditions in labour camp – but which nonetheless radiated joy and love. In fact, this is a characteristic of so many of the faces of Soviet believers. You see a glimpse of heavenly joy mingled with human suffering.

So these were my first experiences of the life of the believers in the Soviet Union. Three months was already beginning to seem far too short a time to find out all that I wanted to about Christians whose lives were an extension of the New Testament.

Church services had been taking place in the home of Vladimir Protsenko since 1973. The believers began to experience harassment from the authorities as soon as it became known where they were meeting. In December 1973 members of the church sent a declaration to Brezhnev protesting about the house searches and confiscation of religious literature which had taken place. Similar declarations were sent in subsequent years, but these protests did nothing to alleviate their suffering. In November 1977 a slanderous article was published in the Leningrad evening newspaper *Vecherni Leningrad*, which accused the pastor of the Leningrad ECB church, Fyodor Makhovitsky, of being involved in 'underhand dealings'. A meeting was called at his place of work and a previously-prepared resolution calling for Makhovitsky to be brought to trial was presented to his workmates. The majority of those present did not vote, but it was announced that the resolution had been carried. Members of the church wrote to Brezhnev in 1978 protesting about this sinister move to start legal proceedings against their pastor on the basis of trumped-up charges.

The net was closing in on Makhovitsky, but it was several years before he was finally arrested. He was detained in August 1981, together with another member of the church, an evangelist named Mikhail Azarov. At the time of the arrest it was reported that they were both being charged under Article 227 of the RSFSR Criminal Code which concerns the organisation and leadership of illegal religious activities. It was also stated that they would face charges under either article 190-1 of the criminal code ('anti-Soviet slander') or Article 190-3 ('creating a public disturbance'). Reporting facts about religious persecution is often construed by the Soviet authorities as 'anti-Soviet slander'. Holding open-air baptisms can be cited as 'creating a public disturbance'.

At the trial which was held from 15–19 February 1982, Makhovitsky (then aged 54) and Azarov (aged 46) were sentenced to five years' strict regime camp and four years' ordinary regime camp respectively. Both were sentenced to a supplementary punishment – confiscation of personal property. Vladimir Protsenko came to trial at the same time, following his arrest in December 1981, and he was sentenced to three years' ordinary regime camp.

Not content with removing three outstanding leaders, the court also ordered that the Protsenko's house should be confiscated, thus intending to terminate the life of the congregation. As it turned out, the congregation was able to continue to meet, because for two years the city authorities took no notice of the court ruling regarding the confiscation of the property. Then in February 1984 they sent Mrs Protsenko instructions to hand over the house and offered her and her three teenage children, still living at home, two flats, one with three rooms and the other with one room. Mrs Protsenko is disabled and receives an invalid pension of 38 roubles (about £35) per month. To make ends meet she is dependent on being able to grow vegetables in her garden. She sent an appeal to the Vsevolzhsk district court explaining her very difficult circumstances and asking for the confiscation order to be revoked. The appeal which was heard on 4th April was rejected. The court justified the decision on the grounds that the house had been extended illegally to provide room for the church to meet for worship. The house had indeed been extended since it was originally built in 1962, but in 1972 the family received permission in principle to extend, then permission to buy a house due for demolition in order to use the building materials. After the work was completed, it was approved by the authorities on 23rd January 1973. However, the court ignored these documents and based its decision on the original plan of 1962.

Seventy-nine members of the Leningrad ECB church appealed to President Chernenko and to the State Procurator General, Rekunkov, to reverse the decision. At the time of writing, the Protsenko family are still living in their house and the church still meets there, but the future is uncertain.

This type of harassment which causes mental anxiety and physical suffering is by no means confined to the Leningrad ECB church in Kuzmolovo. It goes on in the unregistered communities of all denominations all over the Soviet Union.

Had Diana and I known about the fate that was to befall our Christian friends at Kuzmolovo a few years hence, we might have continued to worship with them, but because the house in Kuzmolovo where the church services were held was situated so far from the city centre, it took us almost two hours to get there by train and on foot. This obviously made frequent meetings with our new-found Christian friends impractical. As foreigners we were not, strictly speaking, permitted to travel outside the city limits without express permission. We were sharing rooms in our Leningrad hostel with Russian students who were plainly 'keeping an eye' on us. Although we never attempted to hide the fact that we were going to church, it could have caused problems for the rest of our group if it had become known that we were regularly travelling off limits. These were some of the factors which influenced us in making our difficult decision about where we should go to church. We would have been happy to worship regularly at Kuzmolovo, but decided it would be more practical in the short time we had available to get to know Christians at the registered Baptist church in Leningrad, which was much more accessible. We also knew that if we went to a registered church no awkward questions were likely to be asked.

Our meeting with Valeri on our first visit to the church

at Poklonnaya Gora dispelled any doubts we may have had about the correctness of our choice. Once outside after the service, we were approached by a man in his mid-thirties of medium height with longish straight brown hair and a typically Slav face with high cheek bones. He was wearing Levi jeans and a small metal cross on a chain around his neck. The expression, 'he was grinning from ear to ear' always strikes me as rather far-fetched, but these words were made to describe Valeri's smile which made the skin crease around his eyes. His warmth and friendliness submerged us. We loved his attempts to speak to us in broken English and before long we found ourselves accepting his suggestion that he should accompany us back to our hostel in the centre of the city.

In the tram Valeri spoke freely of his faith and his love for Christ, whom he referred to as 'my Jesus'. He radiated a joy, a zest for life that I had rarely encountered in fellow Christians in Britain. I anxiously looked at the faces of other passengers in the tram to see how they would react to Valeri's public affirmation of the truths of the gospel. By this time he was asking us the translation of certain words: 'How do you say "slava Bogu"? Oh – "Praise the Lord!" ' He savoured the words and repeated them several times.

By this time I was embarrassed and thinking to myself, 'Surely you don't do this kind of thing in public? Least of all in the Soviet Union?' But the faces of the people around me remained impassive. Either they were not interested and were not really listening or they were afraid to betray any emotion. Valeri must have sensed my apprehension. 'I'm not ashamed to talk about my Lord', he said, but without any hint of reproof. This total lack of fear and his spontaneous joy in speaking about 'his Jesus' is characteristic of this extraordinary man and has struck many different people. When he left us, Diana and I could hardly believe what had happened – the impact of this man's personality had stunned both of us equally. We knew that we had come across someone very special.

He invited us warmly to go and visit him and meet his

wife, Tanya, and his two young daughters and gave us directions to his flat. This marked the beginning of a friendship with Valeri and his family which was to draw our lives inextricably together and have extraordinary consequences.

Valeri returned from Western Siberia in 1971. His own brief account gives us a clear indication of the impact of the teaching at the Leningrad church on his life.

On 23rd September 1971 I was baptised and became an active preacher of the gospel. You could say that I became a real Baptist from that point, because earlier I had not known the Bible as I should have done. I had not studied it. In those early years I was allowed to speak from the pulpit, to read spiritual texts to the congregation. But somehow my heart was so full of thanks to God that I could not confine myself just to these activities. I used to add my own insights to the texts, so that in effect I was preaching a sermon.

Who were the leading personalities at the Leningrad Baptist Church at that time and what kind of sermons were they preaching? The best source on this is the one official Baptist publication, *Bratsky Vestnik* (Fraternal Messenger), which by its very nature, as a censored official publication, is not as revealing as it could be. However, it does tell us something of the personalities at the Leningrad church.

The senior presbyter there in the early seventies was Sergei Petrovich Fadyukhin. He was born in 1905 and had lived through many turbulent years in his country's history. He graduated from the Leningrad Bible School in the twenties and emerged as a prominent personality in the mid-fifties. He had spent some years in the Soviet Central Asian republic of Uzbekistan acting as assistant senior presbyter there from 1962. His church was badly affected by the split in Baptist ranks when the Reformers broke away from the AUCECB, but Fadyukhin held firmly to the AUCECB position. At the 1966 All Union

Congress Fadyukhin played a prominent role as assistant general secretary of the Council. He read the official unity report which dealt with the Initsiativniki issue at length. He tried to refute many of the charges made by the Initsiativniki against the AUCECB. Some of his remarks, if they were correctly reported, were certainly unfair and misrepresented the situation of the Reformers, but one must also remember that he would have been under great pressure from the KGB.

Apparently, within the AUCECB, Fadyukhin was advancing rapidly. Within a year of the Congress he was transferred to take over the large Leningrad parish, following the sudden and unexplained death of its young presbyter, A.N. Kiryukhantsev, who had recently returned from studying abroad.

Fadyukhin served in Leningrad until his retirement in 1980. A report appeared in *Bratsky Vestnik* No. 6 (1980) on the 75th Birthday celebration held at the Leningrad Baptist Church in his honour.

From your youth the Lord called you along a narrow and thorny path. He was always with you leading you through sorrows and trials. The Lord uplifted you and comforted you. He was true to all his promises. On the day of your 75th birthday we recognise the many years of pastoral work you have given to the Leningrad church.

Your sermons helped us to grow stronger in the faith and opened to us new depths from the word of God. May God bless you in the coming years of your life and service, for 'the path of the righteous is like the light of dawn which shines brighter and brighter until full day' (Prov. 4.18).

It is probable that this glowing report, to some extent, really reflects the views of members of the congregation, since one of Pastor Fadyukhin's admirers, at least in the early days, was Valeri. He had great respect for Fadyukhin's preaching and was undoubtedly influenced by his sermons. Some of them have been published in *Bratsky Vestnik* and we can judge from this one the kind of teaching Valeri heard Sunday by Sunday as he attended the Leningrad Church (*Bratsky Vestnik* No. 4, 1972, pp.46–9):

Our Lord and Saviour Jesus Christ left on earth a miraculous legacy – his Church. 'The mystery hidden for ages and generations, but now made known to his saints' (Col. 1.26). The Church of Christ is a living organism. The head of the Church is Christ himself. He himself formed it here on earth as a 'pillar and bulwark of truth' (1 Tim. 3.15) and gave to it the blessed Word of Christ, the 'saviour of sinners' (1 Tim. 1.15). It pleased God to make known through the church 'the manifold wisdom of God'. The word 'church' signifies a community. In this case, a community of redeemed souls.

In the Old and New Testaments many promises are given regarding the church. But among them there is one which, like a precious stone, shines down the centuries with the light of the love, kindness and faithfulness of God. The promise is the following: 'The mountains may depart and the hills be removed, but my steadfast love will not depart from you and my covenant of peace shall not be removed, says the Lord. O afflicted one, storm-tossed and not comforted; behold I will set your stones in rubies and lay your foundations with sapphires' (Isa. 54.10–11).

A ruby is a precious stone which reminds us of the colour of Christ's blood. The Apostle Peter, writing to fellow-believers, said, 'You were ransomed not with perishable things such as silver, but with the precious blood of Christ' (1 Pet. 1.18–20). The blood of Christ is like a precious ruby on which the church stands.

A sapphire is also a precious stone, the colour of the

sky. It reminds us that the Church of Christ has a heavenly foundation.

'For no other foundation can anyone lay than that which is laid, which is Jesus Christ' (1 Cor. 3.11). 'And therefore the church is always looking towards things above, its thoughts are on heavenly things' (Col. 3.1–2). If the foundation of the church had been laid with something human or earthly, it would not have withstood the winds and elements of the world. But the church of Christ stands on a firm foundation and its builder is the Lord God himself.

How did the church come into being? The Lord Jesus Christ came to earth and gave the commandment to his disciples: 'Go, therefore, and make disciples of all nations, baptising them in the name of the Father, the Son and the Holy Spirit, teaching them to observe all that I have commanded you' (Matt. 28.19–20). In this command we find the order of creation appointed by the Lord himself. First of all, as the followers of Christ, we are called to instruct people and to take the Gospel message to the world, as it says in the Holy Scripture, 'so faith comes by what is heard and what is heard comes by the preaching of Christ' (Rom. 10.17). When a person hears the Good News, he can either respond and believe or disregard what he hears. If he believes, then according to the word of God he can do no other than repent. For the word of God says all have sinned and fallen short of the glory of God. Whenever a person believed and repented it was then possible for him to be baptised in the name of the Father, the Son and the Holy Spirit.

We believe that those who come to the church in this way are ordained to eternal life, that they are 'no longer strangers and sojourners, but fellow citizens with the saints and members of the household of God, built upon the foundation of the apostles and prophets, Christ

Jesus himself being the cornerstone in whom the whole structure is joined together and grows into a holy temple in the Lord' (Eph. 2.19–21).

Our Lord Jesus Christ, though he came in the flesh as the Son of God, by his nature is 'not of this world' (John 8.23, 42). So too his church, made up of earthly sons and daughters, is not of this world (John 17.16). The life of the church is hidden with Christ in God (Col. 3.3). In expectation of a place in heaven, it continues to inhabit the earth, fulfilling its calling here (Jn. 14.1–3).

In the second half of his sermon, Pastor Fadyukhin emphasises that the right of the church to exercise authority in the world depends on its faithfulness to God and its readiness to abide in Christ, to love God and his word and always to be aware of its dependence on Christ.

He refers to the authority given to members of the church to deal with matters of internal discipline and sin when it is manifested in the lives of believers, but he reminds his readers that the church must not attempt to set itself up as an arbiter of men's souls, for 'Who can forgive sins, but God alone?' He concludes by exhorting his fellow-Christians to live exemplary lives, manifesting Christian virtues at home, at work and in church. He calls on them to show love to one another and to share each others' joys and sorrows. In his sermon Fadyukhin clearly states that it is the responsibility of every follower of Christ to 'take the gospel message to the world'. This exhortation, which Valeri must have heard from the lips of his own pastor on more than one occasion, was to become the dynamo of his life: his joy and his suffering. He simply overflowed with the desire to preach the gospel.

How then did the Baptist leadership react to Valeri? Clearly at the beginning they gave him opportunities to speak, but at the same time they had to be extremely careful about what they could allow. They are ultimately responsible to the Soviet authorities for everything that goes on in every church service. They have to assume that someone from the KGB will be taking notes on every sentence which is uttered in the course of the service. If zealous young men such as Valeri gave up all for the gospel, the pastor would be held responsible. They would be warned by the KGB, but sometimes fines or worse consequences might follow.

People such as Valeri who identify their own spiritual gifts, in his case evangelism, and want to use them in the context of permitted church activities, cannot easily be accommodated within public church life. The authorities' aim is never to relax its grip on any church activities. The simplest way of doing this is to ensure that they have a compliant leadership.

Protestants have no residential seminaries, but the authorities control the admission to seminaries in the Orthodox and Catholic churches and do their best to weed out independent-minded or intellectually outstanding candidates, so that they cannot enter the priesthood. As a result, secret ordinations take place. In the case of the Baptists, the government selects the tiny number of candidates who are to be given the overwhelming privilege of going to study abroad and in return they expect total co-operation from the individuals concerned. The authorities also attempt to control the candidature for the Baptist correspondence courses. Thus some spiritually weaker men rise to positions of authority in the churches and people like Valeri have not the remotest possibility of working openly within the existing church framework without compromising themselves.

However, when Valeri first joined the church he was permitted to take part in the services in the way in which he described. In fact, for the leaders these testimonies provided a useful way of finding out which members of the congregation had potential as preachers.

Reflecting on the period in the early seventies, just after he joined the church, Valeri said:

I learned all the basics of the Christian life and slowly

God was able to deal with all the sinful areas of my life and to correct my faults.

Whatever the problems that may exist within the registered churches, the word of God is powerfully preached in them. It is only when people seek to follow the implications of the word of God uncompromisingly in their lives outside the context of worship that problems arise. Those who are not willing to compromise inevitably end up in conflict with the KGB. Valeri's fate illustrates this tragedy. My own view is that he became a marked man very early on in his ministry, almost certainly without realising the extent to which the unhappy church leadership would eventually betray him.

As Valeri's awareness of the critical situation of the 'politics' in the church sharpened, he inevitably moved further and further outside the sphere of permitted church activities. This brought him into conflict with the church leadership. It is here that we find a paradox. Despite the problems of conscience faced by the Baptist leaders and the effect of their stance on the spiritual health and morale of the rank and file believers, one must acknowledge the transforming power of the Holy Spirit. Valeri would be the first to admit that it was in the Baptist Church, under the teaching and pastoral leadership of men like Sergei Fadyukhin, that he received his real grounding in the Christian faith. This is true of thousands of Baptists who regularly attend registered churches where the Bible is expounded; the gospel is preached, there is a worshipping and a praying community and people's lives are transformed.

How then did Valeri fit into this milieu? Valeri had offered his whole life to God and he is not the kind of man who does things by halves. He was concerned, first and foremost, to follow God's lead, even if it meant doing something in the context of the church which would lead to conflict and which others would find very hard to accept.

Equally important was Valeri's desire to live out the

Christian faith in his society. He had known what it was like to be addicted to alcohol and he had known personally the depth of despair that can drive people to the point of taking their own life. This then motivated him to try to liberate those oppressed by drink and drug abuse with the good news of the gospel and the transforming power of Jesus Christ. He was also concerned for those who filled the spiritual vacuum in their lives with the relentless pursuit of materialism, the compulsion to acquire desirable goods at any price.

The category of oppressed people with which he was most concerned was the young. He wanted to show them that Christian values were worth having and worth living for. But he had a very difficult task. Many of the kids in his neighbourhood led a kind of underworld existence. They were not patriotic, they did not even believe in communism and they drew their enjoyment in life from sex, drugs and alcohol. But Valeri needed a vehicle for proclaiming Christian values. The type of person he wanted to reach would probably never come to church. This is how Valeri described the next stage of his ministry:

I gradually began to realise that the musical ability which God had given me was not being used in his service. It was as if I had buried it. The Lord Jesus seemed to be asking me, 'Why are you not using this talent?' I started to pray earnestly that God would show me how I could employ my musical gifts in my Christian life. Not long afterwards I heard on the radio a Ukrainian-language broadcast of a vocal and instrumental group singing about Jesus Christ.* My immediate reaction was: this is for me. At that time I didn't listen to modern music – I'd given all that up, as I thought, for the sake of God. I'd given away my guitar and other instruments. So you could say I began again from the beginning. I started to pray and the Lord brought me into contact with people I needed. In about 1974 we

* This must have been a Western broadcast.

started to meet at the Lunokhod, the local (Komsomol) youth club at Trinity Fields. We already had people and instruments and we assembled all the necessary equipment. The preparations took a long time because everything was very complicated and we needed a lot of money.

But eventually we formed a good group and its standard was perfectly acceptable for the youth club, where we soon won a fantastic following. . . . It's interesting that just at the time when I got together with this group, through whom I was convinced that God was going to work, we heard the rock opera Jesus Christ Superstar for the first time.* The Lord seemed to reproach me with it. 'You see, the stones cry out but what about you believers? All you do is to gather at the prayer house, sing hymns and psalms and preach. But you despise the sinful world. Who then will save the sinners? If the stones, in other words non-believers, compose such an opera, where does that leave you?' This moved me greatly and as a result I began to fast regularly in order to find out, in the light of this reproach, how to do God's work. And so the group was formed by God. By 1977 we had started to work in earnest at the club and to play at discos. I wanted the young people who played in the band to become believers so that they would have the incentive to practise hard in the hope that eventually, as self-taught musicians, they would turn professional. The whole aim was for us to record our own musical work at some time in the future.

Valeri had by this time written the lyrics of what was to become his rock musical, *The Trumpet Call*, and composed all the music in his head. Diana and I translated the Russian lyrics into English and he began to learn

* Andrew Lloyd-Webber's successful rock musical, performed by non-Christians, was first staged in London in 1971. It was performed in English in the USSR at the Vilnius Conservatory two months *before* it opened in London.

them. We often used to meet him during an off-duty period. He would park the ambulance in a side street and go through all the songs, singing the English vocals at the same time as tapping out the rhythm on the steering wheel and adding special effects!

Valeri had only told the band members about *The Trumpet Call*. The kids at the youth club did not know anything about it. But in the meantime he went, week by week, to play for them. The repertoire was usually Beatles and Rolling Stones numbers which the kids adored. But Valeri was constantly aware of the need to talk to them about Christ.

What was his approach to doing God's work using his musical talent? Firstly it was characterised by prayer and fasting. Secondly he deliberately chose to work with non-Christians and by getting to know them as friends he earned the right to share on a very personal level what Christ meant in his life.

I witnessed the interaction between Valeri and the members of the group in 1977 and their attitude towards him and the values he held was one of great respect. Several of them had taken a first step towards becoming Christians. At the same time they had a brotherly relationship which enabled them to enjoy the time they spent together sharing each other's problems and indulging in hilarious antics together. For example, Vova's father was an alcoholic and his mother depended on him a great deal – he almost became a substitute head of household. Sometimes the responsibility was too much for him – he was only about 19 – and Valeri was always there to encourage and advise him. During rehearsals, Valeri was strict and would get very annoyed if the lads did not concentrate properly or if they just wanted to mess around. After the group had played at a club or a disco, at the end of the evening all the equipment would be piled into Valeri's ambulance – which no doubt Valeri had 'borrowed' for the evening – and the lads climbed in on top. Then the fun would begin. Valeri would take them for a joy ride around Leningrad, seeing how many bridges of the Neva they could cross over and back before they were drawn up at midnight to let the ships pass. They would sing, tell jokes and enthusiastically discuss their next concert.

Valeri's method of evangelism in a wider context among the young people at the club was to build up the human relationships first, to win their trust and friendship and then to share his faith. This was a particular approach adopted at a specific time and accompanied by a great deal of prayer. There were other instances in everyday life, many of which were witnessed by Westerners, including myself, when Valeri spontaneously shared his faith with people he had never seen before in his life. He did not conform to any set pattern or way of doing things – his motto was to be led by the Spirit.

Unfortunately for Valeri, his enthusiasm for reaching young people by means of rock music was not shared by the elders at the Leningrad church or by many of its senior members. Most Baptists in the Soviet Union are extremely conservative and any type of innovation sought by the younger generation is viewed with great suspicion. To use rock music as a means of conveying the gospel was anathema to them.

In order to demonstrate the official Baptist view towards the use of modern music in worship I have translated the article on 'The significance and power of spiritual music' by N.I. Vysotsky, published in the official Baptist Journal, *Bratsky Vestnik*, No. 5 (1978). Vysotsky addresses the important and contentious issue of the *estradnye* (literally 'variety') orchestras, mainly consisting of young people playing modern tunes, and their role in services of worship. Firstly, he is categorical in condemning the influence of jazz in such music.

This music is completely incompatible with the normal spiritual state of a believer's soul because of its excessive loudness, its style and the irreverent manner in which it is performed. Such music provokes irreverence, indignation and protest. One of our well-known church leaders wrote: 'Our singing and music is degenerating. As well as reverent church music, more and more frequently one hears the clanging of cymbals, banging of drums and so on. I must admit that I long for some real choral singing.' In order to deal with these vital and controversial issues Bible courses on the disciplines of singing and music in AUCECB churches have been introduced. The purpose of these courses is to prepare church workers from among our choir leaders who will completely eliminate all the negative aspects of our musical worship of God.

Vysotsky then lists a number of points which are to be given serious consideration. Firstly, he suggests that the term *estradnye* should be dropped because 'variety' orchestras are associated mainly with concert halls and public restaurants and the term is not therefore fitting as a description of an orchestra in the house of God. He suggests that such groups be referred to simply as 'small orchestras'.

Secondly, he states that such orchestras should not be thought of merely as a vehicle for young people to express their feelings. He reminds his readers that during times of worship one is not singing for singing's sake, but to glorify God and urges that all forms of musical 'egoism' be avoided. He points out the necessity for young people to be educated musically so that they develop an appreciation of good spiritual music of a 'high artistic quality'. He recommends that this be achieved by singers and musicians listening to recordings of a selection of high-quality performances during choir practices and rehearsals.

Thirdly, he asks church members to give urgent consideration to the musical repertoire and manner of performance:

Spiritual works of high quality must be introduced into the repertoire and performed whenever possible. Melodies characterised by laboured and jerky rhythms which reflect the lusts of the flesh and mirror empty souls who do not know God must be totally rejected. Spiritual music, like spiritual texts, must be optimistic and joyful, but of course not banal or superficial. Similarly the manner of the performance should be brisk, joyful and spiritual.

Vysotsky then discusses the playing of jazz instruments such as the saxophone and various percussion instruments and recommends that they be banned from use in church. He claims that the use of amplification systems, microphones and so on, distorts both music and the sound of the human voice. Referring to jazz-style rhythms he says the following:

One should avoid such methods of performance as a result of which one's hearing and nerves, but most of all one's spiritual well-being, suffer. This applies both to the performers and the audience. The peace and harmony of the church is disrupted and there is a great victory for temptation. Our Saviour, the Lord Jesus, spoke about the disastrous consequences of this: 'Woe to the man by whom temptation comes' (Matt. 18.7). Temptation can shut the door of one's heart from the word of God and alienate the soul from Christ and from his saving grace.

Finally, Vysotsky warns against the tendency for small groups of instrumentalists and singers to become exclusive and recommends that, as far as possible, there should be close contact and co-operation between all the musicians in the church, so that the 'musical culture' of the whole church is enriched.

In a second article, published more recently in *Bratsky Vestnik* No. 3, 1982, there is a more forthright condemnation of jazz and rock influences in young people's musical groups in church.

In some of our churches, unfortunately, another kind

of music can be heard which bears bitter fruit. It arouses criticism from the listeners and concern and unease among those who serve the churches. I am speaking here of the performances by some variety orchestras and vocal-instrumental groups.

The author claims that electric guitars, played at great volume, exaggerate the rhythm, drown out the words and spoil the melody of a song. The result of such an 'exaggerated' style of performance is to distort the content of songs and distract the attention of the listener. He reminds his readers that Jesus preached with utter simplicity. His parables were accessible to both the ordinary man and the intellectual and His words went forth with conviction because they were spoken in the power of the Holy Spirit. The implication is clear – no gimmick should be used to preach the Word of God.

The author urges his readers not to forget their spiritual heritage or to spoil the musical traditions of the church handed down over decades. His final word is definitely a 'vote of no-confidence' in young Christians aspiring to modernise the evangelical musical repertoire in the Soviet Union:

The rendering of hymns about the suffering of Christ and prayerful psalms with punchy rhythms is simply an insult to the great truths of the Word of God.

'Irreverent' is not an adjective I have heard anyone use to describe Valeri's rock musical, *The Trumpet Call*, but the reader must judge for himself, if he listens to the music. I shall not attempt to describe it myself, though I append the lyrics at the end of the book.

Let us resume Valeri's own narrative at the point where he describes some particular opportunities for evangelism:

After we had been playing for about a year I prayed for an opportunity to hold a discussion at the club about God and the Lord gave me three. It turned out to be very interesting.... All the juveniles were registered with the militia. They could get out of hand. These kids didn't listen to anyone, not even their parents. So, as I said, I had prayed earnestly about this and exactly a year later God gave me an opportunity. How? It was like this. At the end of one of the discos some of the lads came up to me and said, 'Valeri, can you play us something from Superstar?' Our group had already picked up some of the songs from the work, so I immediately replied that we had just started to learn it. At the same time I thought to myself – this is it, this is my opportunity to start up a discussion. I then told the lads that for a long time I'd wanted to have a chat with them about God, about what and who God is and how to understand this phenomenon. I suggested that, if they agreed, we could spend some time discussing this before the next disco. They all responded positively. 'Yes, let's do that, we'd like that.' At that point I knew that if I was summoned by the militia, I would be able to say that the young people themselves had wanted the discussion, that I'd asked them and they had wanted me to tell them about God. So I already had my alibi.

And so the time came for me to try them out. Many of them were smirking and it was obvious that they were not going to believe. I felt embarrassed. Where on earth do I start, I thought to myself. I began my message by talking about the devil. In other words, I told them about the existence of powers of evil, about evil spirits. Suddenly they all started to talk to one another, swopping stories and experiences of the very things I'd been talking about. I then introduced the subject of the Lord and pointed out that just as an evil power exists there is also a power of good.

By the time we had the second discussion they were all sitting with completely serious faces, listening intently. During this discussion it became obvious that we had

80

a KGB agent in our midst. He was wearing civilian clothing, but was obviously much older than the kids – somewhere around thirty years of age. When he had seen that everyone was paying great attention to me he said, 'What are you listening to him for? He's filling your heads with nonsense.' One of the lads who was standing next to him turned to him and said: 'Listen, I came here to learn about life – carry on, Valeri.' So I went on. Later on we had a third discussion and I felt that that was where it must end. That was it – my mission was complete.

Diana and I attended one of the weekly discos and met some of the young people who had earlier become Christians as a result of these 'discussions'. It was obvious that they were very dependent on Valeri to point them along a new path in life. I did not realise it at the time, but this must have placed a considerable strain on him. Every single one of the young people had problems to deal with – some came from broken homes, some, like Vova, had mothers or fathers who were alcoholics. Some had been thrown out of home and were completely cut off from their relatives. They all needed individual counselling and support and this was more than one person could cope with. Valeri did what he could, but often this resulted in tensions at home. Tanya, quite naturally, resented the amount of time he was spending with the young people, because he then neglected helping her with daily chores and spending time with his own children. She was also afraid of the possible consequences of his evangelistic activity.

There was also the problem of integrating these young people into the life of the church. Because they had come to it through Valeri they were regarded by some people with suspicion. He wrote about this to Diana and me because we had met some of the young people.

You know these young people and how difficult it was to teach them and you know how much they loved our group. Well, afterwards when so many of them became believers through the group and then members of the church, I was summoned by the leadership. 'What's all this about? How can this be? Can you be a Christian and play at discos? How is this possible?' It was very difficult for me to explain to them. I told them that you know whether a person is a Christian by the fruit he bears in his life. They could see for themselves: because my work had born fruit, it must be the will of God. This was the point at which a serious conflict arose. Previously I had, as it were, danced to the tune of the pastors, but now I felt the Lord was saying that he alone was my shepherd. When I started to listen to his voice and to follow him, the disagreements emerged. The believers simply didn't understand me. At that time my eyes were opened as never before. I realised that there was a great deal of hypocrisy in our church and that for many people what mattered most was outward appearance, form and ritual, but not the essence of Christianity. So I decided simply to remain firm; to be natural, to be exactly the person God had made me and bravely to stand my ground, even if others didn't understand me. Of course, there were many instances when people came running to me, saying, 'Remove your cross, don't wear jeans'. But I knew that these things were not important. I decided that even if they beat me or tried to crush me, they would only hurt themselves. I would simply hold out and eventually they would understand that these outward things were not important, but what one was like inside.

Some years later, when Valeri was reflecting on this whole episode which caused him such difficulties in the church, he wrote:

When I played at the discos at the youth club, the believers judged me for it. But at the time I thought to myself, 'Which is better: for them (the young people) to be here with me at the club, or left to the mercy of fate?'

When I played at discos, I looked at their faces and prayed for them. Through this prayer God did his work secretly, in other words, he gradually healed their souls.

Some Christians reading this account about Valeri may feel that he should have been willing to conform in his appearance in order not to offend fellow Christians, especially in view of the extreme conservatism of many Soviet Evangelicals. Perhaps Valeri was a little vain. Vanity is after all, a very common human weakness and Christians are by no means exempt from it. Perhaps he wanted to imitate the style of clothing of Western pop idols whose photos he had seen, in order to create an image that would be acceptable to Soviet young people. All young people avidly follow Western fashions, even though it is difficult for them to acquire Western clothing and the kids at the Lunokhod would certainly have expected Valeri to conform to their idea of a pop star. They themselves wore the standard drab, mass-produced clothing churned out by Soviet factories without a single spark of individuality. Literally millions of Soviet citizens under the age of about forty crave for a pair of designer-label Western jeans. The shoddy, shapeless Soviet-made variety simply will not do.

As it happened Valeri was fortunate enough to possess one pair of blue jeans and he had a weakness for American sweatshirts. But his appearance was by no means way out, as many photographs of him show. He did once mention to me that when his group had made their recording of *The Trumpet Call* he would have T-shirts printed with the words 'Trumpet Call' blazoned across the front. (Trumpet Call T-shirts have been printed in the West, but not, of course, in the Soviet Union.) In Western pop culture this is the norm. The whole question of Valeri's external appearance became, apparently, an issue of great importance, because it was eventually given as one of the pretexts for expelling him from the Baptist church. But this is jumping ahead.

My own view is that, if those who criticised Valeri had not been able to find fault with his appearance, they would have found some other pretext for condemning him. However, if I have given the impression that Valeri's supporters came only from the ranks of the young people, I must immediately correct this.

One afternoon I attended an unofficial prayer meeting held at the home of one of the women who attended the Baptist church. I have a clear memory of the flat with its narrow hallway, half filled with a coat stand bulging with outdoor garments – woolly hats and scarves and numerous pairs of stout outdoor shoes lined up against the wall. There was always a distinctive smell which seemed to penetrate from the kitchen; perhaps it was cabbage soup mixed with the musty smell which came from the old, worn upholstery in the living room. Through the bedroom door which was left ajar I caught a glimpse of a high, old-fashioned four-poster bed piled high with more coats, hats and scarves.

The living room was crowded with people, mainly *babushki* (old women), many of them wearing black. Almost all had their heads covered with brightly patterned head scarves. They were nearly all overweight and this made the room seem even fuller. Someone had brought in long wooden benches and so everyone had a place to sit, but as the prayer meeting got underway these dear old ladies got down on their knees. Some men were present, including Valeri, and some young people. The intensity of prayer was the same as among the unregistered Baptists. Many of the women broke into sobs as they pleaded with God and it was impossible for me, too, to remain dry-eyed. By this time, my comprehension of Russian had improved considerably, but I still found it difficult to concentrate on people's prayers and my mind wandered. I was unused to remaining on my knees for more than ten minutes at a time and the growing ache in my back also distracted me.

84

But suddenly my ears pricked up. I had heard the words *Trubny Zov* – the Trumpet Call – or was I imagining it? No, one of the women was actually praying for Valeri and his rock musical. I opened my eyes in disbelief. Then the theme was taken up by several others in succession and the prayers were heartfelt. They were asking God to bless Valeri's work among young people and thanking God that he had given Valeri a special way of communicating with them. They prayed that Valeri would remain strong and single-minded in his goal, despite any opposition he would have to face.

There were many ordinary members of the congregation who loved Valeri and supported him. They have defended him in the way they knew to be most effective – through prayer – and their prayers have had, at times, remarkable effect.

Having made his decision to follow what he considered to be God's prompting, and not to be intimidated by the Baptist leadership, Valeri began a new phase in his life:

From the end of 1977, after you went back to the UK, I experienced the most terrible difficulties in church. People didn't understand me and started to reject me. When the question arose of who should become the leader of the young people's work in church someone put forward my name. But they (the leadership) said: 'Valeri Barinov? Is he a believer?' So I was maligned in front of everyone. But I took no notice and put my trust in God. Then all at once some of the really talented lads in the group were called up to do their army service and I was left without any gifted musicians. I felt I had no base of support.

To lose the key members of the group was obviously a great blow to Valeri. It destroyed his hopes of being able to record *The Trumpet Call*. I am sure that it made him question his motives and wonder whether, after all, he had misinterpreted God's guidance. Although he writes that he did not take any notice of the criticism levelled against him by some of the church authorities, it obviously had a very damaging psychological effect. He was being frustrated on all sides in his attempts to minister to young people.

It was at this particular time that he first began to think about the possibility of emigrating to the West. He knew that he and his family would not be allowed to emigrate legally (only people with relatives abroad could do that), so he began to think of various schemes to escape from the Soviet Union. It is important to understand his frame of mind. People in desperate situations are driven to take desperate measures. Valeri had always had a romantic dream about being able to go on tour and perform Christian music in the West. He had firmly promised that he and the family would come to see Diana and me in the UK. Of course, we were tempted to indulge in wishful thinking, but we tried to be realistic and explain to Valeri that this really was just a dream. 'Ah, but with God, anything is possible', he always added as the last word. The fact that Valeri had committed the crime of thinking, talking and writing about his desire to leave the country would eventually be part of his downfall. In the Soviet Union, if you want to leave your country there must be something wrong with you; either you are mentally ill or you are a criminal or a traitor.

If the Soviet Union were to open up its borders literally millions of people would emigrate and tens of millions would travel to see other countries. There are countless tragic stories of ordinary people, many of them religious believers, who have given up hope of winning their religious rights and have wasted years of their lives in a futile battle with the Soviet authorities trying to obtain permission to emigrate. The Soviet Union has signed covenants in international law which guarantee freedom of religion, of travel and much else. In 1975 these were underlined by the Helsinki Accords, which emphasised the international monitoring of human-rights performance. Therefore Valeri was asking for nothing beyond his legal rights and it is not his fault that the Soviet government constantly violates agreements into which it has freely entered.

One must bear in mind that ordinary Soviet citizens are kept in almost total ignorance about the regulations and formalities required when one travels abroad. Why should they be told, since only the privileged class in Soviet society is permitted to travel abroad outside the Eastern block? Similarly, with regard to the patrolling of the Soviet border, the average citizen would have little idea, except from hearsay, about the massive security operation which ensures that Soviet citizens do not escape (although some do). Many have tried and failed and ended up in labour camp. Some, like Valeri, have thought about it, decided not to attempt it and still ended up in labour camp.

How can Soviet citizens possibly find out about border security? Such information is guarded jealously, as if it were a state secret, and as an ordinary citizen you cannot read about it anywhere. Some information, of course, is passed on by word of mouth. Naturally the border guards talk and they know something – how many patrols, mine fields, watch towers, barbed wire perimeter fences and how many packs of guard dogs, but on the whole not many people know the details.

Soviet citizens are deliberately kept in total ignorance about even the most basic facts of Soviet life. There are whole categories of information which are forbidden to the public or which are made available only in heavily-censored and controlled doses. It is very rare indeed, for example, for the Soviet media to report on any type of catastrophe, except when it occurs outside the Soviet block. You will hardly ever read in the Soviet press reports of air crashes, explosions, earthquakes or floods that have taken place on Soviet territory. Again, this kind of information is spread by word of mouth from eye witnesses, but inevitably the true facts are distorted along the way.

So we should not be surprised at Valeri's apparent naivety, or some may say, stupidity. I do not think it would be fair to say that Valeri believed he could make a successful escape attempt simply because God was on his side. His initial optimism was based largely on ignorance. When, several years later, he learned from a Western visitor some of the hard facts about border controls and passport regulations, he was astounded. But he never dismissed the possibility completely from his mind. At the same time he did make enquiries with his Western friends about any legal method of emigrating from the Soviet Union and requested that an invitation be sent to him and his family from the West. Often the invitations sent from abroad never reach the person concerned. They are simply confiscated by the authorities.

How then did Valeri resolve these immediate difficulties and overcome his fear, and what finally prevented him during those troubled years from trying out one of his reckless schemes to leave the country? Despite his feeling of despair, of having momentarily lost his sense of direction, Valeri continued to pray for guidance. At the beginning of 1980 God intervened in a remarkable way and at this point another Western Christian, an American, entered Valeri's life. Before recounting this episode, I want first of all to return to 1977 when I met Valeri and Tanya to give a portrait of the Barinov household as I saw it and then move on to 1982 when I visited them for the second and last time.

5: At home

In 1977 the Barinovs lived in one of the many large grey
blocks of dingy communal flats which are a feature of the
inner residential areas of the city. The six-storey buildings
were grouped around three sides of a rectangle with a
central area of grass and trees which was always littered
with empty bottles and smelt like a public lavatory. The
children in the neighbourhood used this as a play area and
in the summer evenings you could hear the shouts of a
group of boys playing football. Valeri and Tanya and the
two girls lived in one room and shared a small kitchen
and toilet with the occupants of the other two rooms in
the ground-floor flat. The communal kitchen was at the
front of the block with a window looking onto the grassy
play area and was the sunniest room. The Barinovs' own
room was at the back and from their window all you could
see was a yard with a broken down fence separating their
block of flats from the adjoining one. The path running
along the back of the whole block of flats was overgrown
with weeds and the grass was high. The kitchen contained
a cooker, a sink with a cold tap, cupboards for cooking
utensils and a small table. There was no bathroom. Tanya
kept a tin bath for the two girls, but in flats where there
is no bathroom people simply go to the public bath house
and this was a weekly ritual in the Barinov household, as
it has been for generations of other Russians. The Barinovs' room was long, narrow and dark. It contained two
settees which opened out into beds, a small table and
chairs, a refrigerator, a cabinet containing glass and china
and displaying family photographs, an attractive hand-

woven carpet hung on one wall, a television and a record player.

I had become used to living in fairly primitive conditions in the Soviet Union. My particular group of students was housed in a nineteenth-century hostel on Mytninskaya Naberezhnaya, conveniently situated in the centre of Leningrad. The hostel was in a magnificent setting, but did not have much to offer in the way of creature comforts. There were five of us sharing a room, three British and two Russian students. However, we did have access to women's communal showers and at certain times of the week there was hot water. Apart from the individual wooden houses which I had seen out in the suburbs of the city where the unregistered Baptists held their meetings, I had not seen an average family home. In my middle-class upbringing I had always lived in a spacious family house with my own bedroom. I remember being horrified when I first saw the Barinovs' flat and I could hardly believe that four people could be expected to live in such cramped and primitive conditions. The Soviet Union is not, after all, a third-world country. The Barinovs' situation was by no means untypical of millions of ordinary Soviet citizens. In the country you may have more space, but many consumer items are unobtainable and the supply of goods to remote areas is extremely erratic.

In his book *Nomenklatura*, Michael Voslensky has presented a comprehensive picture of the Soviet class system. He describes how the Soviet Union came to be ruled by a monopolistic, privileged sect, the Nomenklatura, how this group has gained supremacy, legalised its position and held firmly on to the reins of power since the Revolution. Voslensky was himself a member of the Nomenklatura, a high-ranking official and a historian who left the Soviet Union in 1972. In his book he describes the two different worlds of the exploited and the privileged class and draws comparisons between the lot of the ordinary Soviet citizen and that of a member of the ruling élite.

What he says about housing bears out my own observation about the Barinovs' accommodation being the norm:

> For the population at large the housing problem is so acute that it is actually admitted by the authorities. Party and government resolutions, and speeches and articles in the press, agree that, while Soviet citizens enjoy all the good things of life, the exception is the housing problem, which has not yet been satisfactorily solved. 'Activity on a gigantic scale' is of course taking place in the building sector, and with every day that passes every citizen has a better chance of improved living conditions. Nevertheless the target announced at the beginning of the sixties, that every citizen should have a room to himself, is still far from having been reached. The Soviet norm is nine to twelve square meters of habitable space per person. In the West, as I have had occasion to note, that figure is generally not understood, or is taken to apply to a bedroom.

> And particularly rare are those who understand that twelve square meters of habitable space in excess of the norm was formerly simply confiscated, and in 1984 the rent was tripled. An area of about five square meters per person is considered to be a kind of minimum though it is not guaranteed. A family living in those conditions is considered to be 'in a situation of distress in the housing sector' and is put on the waiting list of the housing service of the district soviet. The wait is generally a long one.

Valeri told us that he had been on the waiting list for rehousing for three years and he expected to be able to move to a larger flat within the next three years. In fact, the family was rehoused at the end of 1979 into a much more spacious flat containing two bedrooms, a living room and a small kitchen and bathroom. By contrast, let us see what Voslensky has to say about the housing of the privileged class:

Housing for the Nomenklatura is built under special supervision and is not standardized or jerry-built. Good, solid buildings contain spacious apartments, quiet elevators, wide and comfortable staircases. . . . The times have passed when victorious Communist workers emerged from their cellars to install themselves in the homes of the wealthy. Aristocratic homes and districts have reappeared under the real-socialist regime, and carefully selected workmen have access to them only to carry out repairs.

These homes are large; they may have as many as eight rooms. Especially important Nomenklaturists may be allotted a whole floor, consisting of two adjoining flats turned into one. . . .

In an over-populated city like Moscow, with its 7.6 million inhabitants (1975), the situation is acute, and the waiting lists of persons admitted to be in a situation of distress in the housing sector, that is, having less than five square meters each at their disposal, are never-ending. In spite of that, the Moscow average is fifteen square meters per person, or more than double that of the rest of the country. This is explained by the large number of Nomenklaturists living in the capital. Their spacious apartments make it appear on paper to be the best-off city in the Soviet Union so far as housing is concerned.

Taking into account the habitable space actually available, an average Moscow family of four ought to be occupying an apartment of sixty square meters now, and not in a radiant Communist future. The causes of the Moscow housing crisis are not technical, but social. If the inhabitants of Moscow live in such overcrowded conditions, it is not because the habitable space available in Moscow is too small, but because the Nomenklatura occupies too much of it, at the expense of workers who have been on a waiting list and have been living with their families in single rooms for years.

The fact that their rulers enjoy such privileges is well known to the ordinary citizen. On one occasion when Valeri was off duty he gave us a guided tour of a part of Leningrad we had never seen before. He drove us in the ambulance to what appeared to be the edge of an attractive, landscaped park, well fenced off from the road. In the distance surrounded by mature trees, we could see a large building which, while not distinguished architecturally, was markedly more attractive than the average blocks of residential flats which somehow gave the impression of decay. By contrast this building was solid looking and well maintained. I remember noticing that the windows gleamed. Valeri pointed out rows of television aerials on the roof of the building. 'They probably have a colour TV in every room' was his wry comment. When we expressed our astonishment at this glaring discrepancy in the standard of accommodation, Valeri simply shrugged and told us that this was a fact of life in a communist society.

As it was, the tiny flat in Babushkin Street became a second home for Diana and me and I still feel a curious affection for it. We became, albeit for a short time, members of the family. Over the three months we spent numerous hours with the Barinovs, sharing family meals, playing with the children, meeting relatives, friends and neighbours and hearing all the local gossip, joining in family outings and celebrations such as Tanya's birthday. All these experiences combined to make those three months in the Soviet Union one of the happiest periods of my life. I was a visitor and this was a pleasant interlude in my studies and it was not until much later that I was to find out more about the sad fate of victims of the Soviet system. At that time I could not possibly have imagined that Valeri and his family were to become such victims.

In the evenings when Zhanna and Marina, then aged seven and six respectively, were going off to sleep, we often used to sit in the kitchen when it was not being used by the other occupants of the flat. The last rays of the evening sun glinted through the open window where Valeri would be perched on the sill, guitar in hands. Tanya and Valya, Valeri's cousin, used to teach us Russian folk songs and for all of us it was a very simple but enjoyable way of spending time together. On other occasions Valeri used to play records of Western rock music. He was very proud of this collection which he had painstakingly acquired over a number of years. The influence of some of the groups, hugely popular in the early seventies, such as Pink Floyd, can clearly be heard in Valeri's own composition. He was particularly interested in music by Western Christian artists and Cliff Richard has remained one of his heroes and someone whose example he always wished to follow.

Tanya with her lovely red hair and green eyes immediately drew one's attention. She had a pale, clear complexion, but her fine features were marred by a deep scar just to the right of her chin. She was reluctant to tell us the story, but apparently when she was a teenager there had been an accident with a gun and the bullet hit the side of her face.

She always welcomed us, but could never really disguise the fact that she was tired and overworked. She had a full-time job in a factory – in the Soviet Union women are an essential part of the workforce – and two demanding children to look after, not to mention a husband who was, to say the least, unpredictable. Whenever Valeri was around he dominated all the conversation and attention was drawn irresistibly to him. At such times I felt that Tanya, quite understandably, had a certain resentment to our being there. When we did have Tanya to ourselves, on visits to the cinema or outings with the children, she was very curious to find out about all aspects of life in Britain. We discussed a whole range of topics from the Royal Family – it was the year of the Queen's Silver Jubilee – to the problem of unemployment, to fashions and hair styles.

We were often aware of the tension that existed in the marriage. Tanya was frequently very critical of Valeri and her chief complaint was the amount of time he spent at church and on evangelistic work. Tanya was by no means hostile to Christianity, but for her at that time it was a private matter between God and the individual. She could not understand Valeri's evangelistic zeal. She was a down-to-earth person of great integrity and I think she felt that if people lived according to their conscience they would instinctively obey God and keep his commandments. If they did not and as a result led lives of immorality and wickedness, then they would deserve whatever fate was coming to them. Valeri's attitude could not have been more diametrically opposed to hers. Christ had rescued him from utter degradation and for Valeri no one was beyond hope. In Valeri's neighbourhood there was plenty of evidence of people of all ages with severe domestic problems and the root cause of many of these ills was alcoholism. This was a phenomenon about which I had been totally ignorant before I arrived in the Soviet Union.

In the backstreets behind the student hostel where I was living there were a number of small shops where I used to buy bread, milk and the other limited groceries available. A few days after I had arrived on my first ever trip to a communist country, I was exploring these backstreets and was astonished to see an enormous queue of people forming outside what appeared to be a grocery store at about three o'clock in the afternoon. 'Oh well,' I thought, 'the Russians obviously have long lunch breaks and these people must be anxious to get their shopping done as soon as the shop reopens.' It did strike me as very odd that such a large number of people were evidently absent from work in the middle of the afternoon.

As I walked by and took a closer look, I noticed how unattractive these people were. They had an air of world weariness. This is not surprising in view of the amount of time Russians have to spend waiting in queues. They appeared unhealthy with pale, worn faces and shapeless figures not enhanced by drab, ill-fitting clothes. On my way back from my walk about half an hour later the shop had reopened but the queue had not dispersed. It was then that I noticed that they were all waiting at a separate entrance to get to a special counter at the far end of the store. This counter was divided off from the rest of the shop by a glass door and screen. I stood in the main part of the shop where groceries were displayed and peered through into the other section. Then I noticed what was on sale there – alcohol.

It was an extraordinary sight. Faces which had appeared almost dazed with weariness had suddenly become animated. People were elbowing their way forward to reach the counter. Voices were raised in anger as some people jumped the queue. A scuffle broke out and the sales assistant, a woman in her thirties, yelled in fury at the two men who were jostling each other. I couldn't understand what she said, but I could tell by her face and tone that it wasn't very pleasant. Eventually two men appeared from a door somewhere at the rear of the counter and hustled the two offenders outside. The atmosphere was ugly and threatening. Violence was only a little below the surface. I watched for a few minutes as bottles of beer, wine and vodka were handed over the counter in endless succession and people hurried away, presumably back to work or to go and drink quietly somewhere. Absentmindedly I walked past the cash desk where a middle-aged lady in a grubby white overall was busily adding up the cost of someone's purchases on an abacus. I still had the empty wire shopping basket in my hand as I approached the exit.

Suddenly, someone let out another yell and this time I was the one who was in trouble. The cashier came in hot pursuit accusing me of trying to steal state property. Overcome with embarrassment I thrust the basket into her hands and tried to explain in halting Russian that it was a mistake. She insisted on searching my shoulder bag to see if I had picked up something without paying for it before she let me leave the shop.

The queue formed every day and I gradually became aware of the fact that heavy drinking is part of the way of life in the Soviet Union. A very large proportion of the average monthly wage is spent on alcohol. In this respect, Valeri's former drinking habits were the norm.

A revealing article appeared in the West German newspaper *Die Zeit* in January 1985. It was based on a report by Milan Dragovic, Moscow correspondent of Agence France Presse. Here are some extracts from it:

Researchers at the Soviet Academy of Sciences in Novosibirsk have written a confidential report on alcohol abuse in the Soviet Union for the leadership of the Communist Party. They describe the abuse of alcohol in their report as 'the greatest tragedy of our thousand year history'. Every sixth child in the Soviet Union is born mentally handicapped or with a hereditary illness.

According to statistics quoted by the Soviet research centre in 1980, 40 million Soviet citizens were officially registered as heavy drinkers or alcoholics, that is every sixth inhabitant of the Soviet Union. Of these, the number of chronic alcoholics is estimated at 17 million. The other 23 million are heavy drinkers whose condition is not yet pathological. Every year a million people perish as a result of excessive alcohol consumption. 'The result of this addiction is a systematic degeneration of the nation, and in particular the Russian population. Who needs to declare war against us if in twelve or fifteen years' time we fall apart? We are a sovereign state, more than half of whose adult population consists of alcoholics and heavy drinkers who are incapable of working or defending themselves.' Consumption of vodka is increasing constantly. In 1952 the annual per capita consumption was five litres. In 1983 it was 30 litres. If this trend continues, by the year 2,000 the statistical average for each Soviet citizen will be 50 litres of vodka per year, in other words, 20 litres of pure alcohol. The country would then have 60 million addicts and regular drinkers.

The Novosibirsk researchers illustrated the continuing degeneration of the population by quoting the increase in the number of institutes set up to care for mentally handicapped children. They document this trend only up to the year 1975 because the most recent figures, they claim, are too compromising. But they quote the director of a pedagogical institute who stated that 16.5 per cent of children born in 1982 were mentally subnormal – every sixth newborn child. As an example, statistics for the Donetsk region in Ukraine are quoted. In 1960 there were four schools in this region for mentally handicapped children; today there are 38.

The Soviet state earns an annual revenue of 45 billion roubles from the sale of vodka. The Soviet economy loses 80 billion roubles annually as a result of alcoholism. A survey carried out in 1979 revealed that 99.4 per cent of Soviet men, 97.6 per cent of Soviet women and 95 per cent of adolescent girls under the age of 18 regularly drink alcohol. The newspaper *Selskaya Zhizhn* (Country Life) reported, according to *Die Zeit*, that 90 per cent of the people who have undergone 'cures' for drink problems are, at the time of their first 'cure', under fifteen years of age and a third are under ten years of age. In 85 per cent of cases of murder, rape, theft and burglary, alcohol abuse is said to be the cause of the crime.

The researchers paint a very black picture of the inhabitants of Siberia where there is hardly a single driver of agricultural machinery who reaches the pensionable age of 60. The compilers of the report end with the satirical remark that to meet a sober Siberian in the evening is like meeting a man from Mars.

It is hardly surprising in the light of the above that in the Trinity Fields housing district we encountered a number of pathetic cases who were badly in need of a cure. One of the local 'characters' was Sergei and the contrast between Valeri's and Tanya's attitude to this man illustrates very clearly the very different views they held about Christianity at that time.

Sergei was a notorious drunkard and womaniser. Many people feared him because when he was drunk he became violent and many of the women in the neighbourhood, Tanya included, despised him. He was a huge man with powerful shoulders, a heavy jutting jaw and enormous fists. His narrow eyes gave him a menacing appearance even when he was sober.

Valeri's heart went out to Sergei. He tried to reason with him, he lent him money which was never repaid and he never missed an opportunity to share the gospel with him. One of the consequences was that when Sergei was rolling drunk and had run out of money for the next bottle of vodka he came knocking on the Barinovs' door. Tanya never let him in the flat, sober or otherwise, but Valeri never refused him. This did not stop Sergei from venting his frustration and rage about life on Valeri, if he happened to be in the mood, and on more than one occasion he put his great fist through the Barinovs' window. Fortunately, he never attacked Valeri physically.

I did not know many Russian swear words, but Valeri told me that Sergei's language made even him, though he thought he had heard it all in the army, draw a deep breath. Tanya used to be furious with Valeri for having anything to do with Sergei and warned him that one day she or one of the girls would become one of his victims. In the end Valeri gave up the hopeless task of trying to reason with this giant, but he still continued to pray for him.

Tanya sometimes went to the Leningrad Church with Valeri, but never felt really comfortable there. The judgmental attitudes which she encountered tried her patience to the limits. Probably she was resentful of the way in which Valeri was being treated by some of the Baptist leaders. Despite her opposition to some of Valeri's activities, she has demonstrated loyalty and devotion to him through painful and uncertain years. Valeri was obviously used to Tanya's standard reaction to his 'work for the Lord' because he was able nearly always to win her round to his way of thinking.

Valeri has an extraordinary ability to gain people's sympathy and he would have made a successful actor had he had the opportunity. If Tanya proved to be unyielding in her anger or criticism, Valeri would appeal to his two daughters to defend him against Tanya's sharp tongue and the whole episode would be turned into an enormous joke. The girls would defend papa, but at the same time remonstrate with him and soon everyone would be laughing. Living in such a confined space, they acted out the traumas and dramas of family life on a central stage. Perhaps the fact that people cannot easily get away from one another contributes to a certain malaise in Soviet society and is one of the several contributory factors to the problem of alcoholism.

Tanya was initially critical of Valeri's musical ventures, although in subsequent years she changed her mind when she witnessed the impact of the Trumpet Call group on young people. She dismissed the whole idea of recording *The Trumpet Call* as a wild fantasy. I must admit that I shared her view. I wanted to believe that it would be possible, but I thought it unlikely. Consequently, whenever Valeri tried to tell Tanya about a new idea for a song or a new musical arrangement she humoured him but did not show any real enthusiasm. She was afraid of the risks he was taking by playing at the Lunokhod and openly witnessing there and became very angry when her attempts to make him stop failed. She knew what the repercussions for family life would be if Valeri got into serious trouble and her first instinct was to protect Zhanna and Marina.

Valeri's stock answer was 'The Lord will look after you'. He, of course, firmly believed this and did not say it glibly, but it made Tanya furious. We felt great sympathy for Tanya and understood her point of view, but at the same time we could see the potential of Valeri's ministry among the lost youth. If Diana and I tried to put

100

Tanya's position to Valeri, hoping that he might respect what we had to say, he would round on all three of us and preach a mini-sermon telling us that Christ's command to his disciples was to go and preach the gospel to the whole world and that this was the most important mission in his life. Diana and I were, after all, translating the lyrics of *The Trumpet Call* so that Valeri's music could reach an English-speaking audience. How could we fault his zeal?

It was not until several years later when I saw Tanya on a return visit to Leningrad in 1982 that I began to realise fully what an enormous price she had paid for Valeri's activities in terms of a secure and happy family life. However, in the five intervening years Tanya had become committed to Valeri's work with the Trumpet Call group and actively supported it, both morally and in practical ways. For example, six members of the group, including Valeri, had been rehearsing secretly on the morning I called to see Tanya and they all turned up at the flat around midday. Tanya immediately got to work and provided a substantial meal for all of them and the Barinov income at that time was well below average.

On that occasion I asked Tanya privately whether she resented the fact that Valeri had put his Christian witness before his family life. Tanya replied that she considered herself very fortunate in having a husband like Valeri. 'There are so many hopeless marriages, drunken husbands who hardly do a day's work from one month to the next and what little money they bring home is spent on drink. Yet they are left alone to make public nuisances of themselves. But Valeri, who has always been hardworking and honest, is victimised and penalised just because he's a Christian with integrity and high ideals. Of course, our family life is disrupted, but I must support him along the path he's chosen.' Her eyes filled with tears.

Valeri had already been sacked from his job as an ambulance driver and was working as a stoker. He had to shovel coal into a furnace which heated a huge apartment block. In typical Valeri fashion, he did an instant mime of what his life as a stoker was like, until we all collapsed with laughter. He described the two *babushki* with whom he worked and to whom he was constantly witnessing. 'One of them is a good woman, an Orthodox believer,' he said, 'the other thinks I'm mad, but I can tell that she likes me! I've given her a New Testament and she's reading it!' Valeri had been working all the previous night and had come home at about six in the morning. He had snatched a few hours' sleep and then gone straight off to a rehearsal.

'You see how good the Lord is,' he said. 'He provides me with a job that I can do at night so that I'm free for His work during the day. And those two old women, they won't tell the management about me, so I won't get the sack.'

'But Valeri, when do you sleep?' I protested. 'Oh, we take it in turns to stoke the fire. While they stoke, I sleep and in any case, I think I will soon be able to do the job in my sleep.' With that he indulged in another mime of an idiot-faced stoker, eyes closed, shovelling fuel into a furnace and stripping off layers of imaginary clothing as he did so.

Over the years there were many happy family occasions which compensated for shortage of money, poor living conditions and uncertainty about the future. After all, if you cannot change your circumstances you have to make the best of them. This must be the motto of millions of Soviet citizens living under communism. In many Soviet families children are a focus of attention, objects of lavish affection, and the Barinov household was no exception. Both girls adored their parents. Zhanna was a boisterous tomboy and had an especially close relationship with her father. Marina has a quieter temperament and a more timid nature. When I first knew them they were simply pretty little girls with huge ribbons in their hair, full of life and affection. On my subsequent visit they were aged 12 and 11, had developed their personalities more distinctively and were eager to communicate. They were used to foreign visitors because by that time Valeri had made many contacts with Westerners who came to the Baptist Church in Leningrad.

I spent several delightful hours alone one morning with Zhanna and Marina while Tanya was at work and Valeri was at the rehearsal. First of all, I showed them some family photographs and they, in turn, showed me some of their valued possessions; scrap books, stamp collections and picture postcards of which they insisted on giving me several. They politely corrected my Russian then laughed at my repeated mispronunciations, interpreted a wildlife programme on TV and made me tea. Zhanna was particularly curious to know about my step-son, Mark, who was then aged 14. Mark had sent a few of his old story books to help them with their English and they immediately collected together some badges and postcards for me to take back for him and Zhanna even wrote him a short note.

When Valeri came home it soon became obvious that his relationship with the girls was as close and tender as it has always been. He still delighted them with his mad acting and jokes. On this occasion he performed a whole series of tricks with the family pet, a large, sleek black dog called Panterka. This involved rolling himself into a tight ball and instructing the dog to leap over him. Panterka was then rewarded with food by all the members of the family.

On the next day I called to say goodbye to the family as I was leaving that afternoon to fly back to England. They presented me with a large cardboard box. Tanya said, 'We wanted to give you a present but we weren't sure what to buy. Valeri has been out to choose it this morning. We hope you like it.' It was an electric table lamp in the style of an old-fashioned oil lamp. I was overwhelmed. It was only when I got back to my hotel room and dismantled the lamp in order to pack it carefully that I discovered the 'guarantee' form with the price stamped on the back. It had cost a hundred roubles – the equivalent of a month's salary. This was typical of their great generosity.

One of the things I took home with me following my brief visit to Leningrad was a list of items of musical equipment which Valeri needed. By that time, plans for recording *The Trumpet Call* were well under way. What he required most urgently was a synthesiser and he had even written down the exact model he wanted, having seen it advertised in a copy of *Melody Maker*. This was disconcerting, because I could not imagine how such a substantial item of equipment could be brought through Soviet customs without arousing great suspicion. And whom was I going to persuade to take it in? Valeri simply said, 'Pray about it.'

That story will be told later, but first of all I must go back and fill in what had happened in the intervening years since 1980 when Valeri had begun to have doubts about God's calling to him to be a rock'n'roll youth evangelist in Leningrad.

6: Help from outside

My friend Tim has told the remarkable story of his encounter with Valeri in his own words. When I received his manuscript and read it through, it gave me great pleasure to know that my subjective assessment of Valeri's character and personality is shared, in almost every detail, by others. Valeri has been much maligned in the Soviet press, by Soviet officials and by Baptist leaders in the Soviet Union, and I hope that this account will help set the record straight.

Tim is currently actively involved in promoting Valeri's music in the United States. Here is his story in his own words:

My first recollection of hearing the name of Valeri Barinov came while visiting Mike Rowe one day at Keston College before a trip to Moscow and Leningrad. I was making preparations for gospel musicians to visit the Soviet Union. Mike gave me Valeri's name and address and asked if I would visit him while in Leningrad. He told me that Valeri was a Christian musician who wanted to witness through rock music. Mike also indicated that he and others didn't know quite how to advise Valeri, as they weren't musicians themselves, so they asked me to talk to him.

I planned to visit Leningrad on my way back to Moscow before leaving the country at the end of the two-week trip. On arrival in Leningrad I was assigned to a hotel and after dinner I looked for a way to leave the hotel to visit Valeri without being followed. Few pedestrians passed the hotel, so it was easy to see who was leaving and the main access was by car.

I finally decided simply to start walking, as though looking at the sights. Then I began to look for a taxi without a radio antenna. I knew that many Leningrad taxis were being fitted with radios to keep tabs on tourists expected for the 1980 Olympics.

At about ten forty-five p.m., somewhere not far from the centre of Leningrad, I finally managed to hail a radio-less taxi. After a prolonged search up several blind alleys, we pulled up in front of number nine and the driver pointed to the door. The flat was on the ground floor so it took no more than a minute to find the door. By now it was almost midnight. I knocked. About 20 seconds later I heard a faint 'Da', but the person didn't open the door. I asked, 'Is Valeri Barinov there?'... There was no answer. I guessed that whoever was there didn't speak English, so I simply repeated, 'Valeri Barinov?' The reply from behind the door was another faint, 'Da'. I waited for about 15 seconds for a response, but still the door was not opened. I repeated, 'Valeri Barinov', but this time there was no response.

I decided to leave a message, just in case Valeri was out and might possibly return before I left the next afternoon. I scrawled a note telling him briefly that I was a friend of Mike Rowe and left the hotel name and my room number. I wedged the note into the door jamb, returned to the taxi and arrived back at the hotel at about one o'clock. By now I was resigned to not meeting Valeri on this trip.

At about six-thirty next morning my phone rang. I picked up the receiver and the voice on the other end of the line said, 'Hello, Tim, this is Valeri Barinov.' I asked him where he was and he told me that he was phoning from a call box near the hotel and would walk over to meet me. I asked him to give me half an hour to dress and then I'd meet him outside.

My past experience with meeting believers had taught me never to meet at a hotel entrance because of the KGB snoopers who always hang around outside. But Valeri disregarded this by his own choice and met me outside as agreed.

Valeri has an infectious grin and a gregarious personality, full of enthusiasm and zest. His first words to me, a total stranger to him, were 'Hello, Tim. Praise the Lord.'

We walked about three hundred yards and then turned into the courtyard of an old high-rise block of flats where Valeri had parked his work vehicle, an ambulance. We sat in it for a while just to get acquainted. He was overjoyed to see me and especially to talk with a fellow musician who was a believer. I'll never forget one expression Valeri used repeatedly – it was 'My Jesus' whenever he referred to the Lord. Valeri told me a little about the band he had formed and how they had been trying to do evangelistic work. Valeri's job put him in touch almost every day with the down-and-outs in Leningrad. He seemed to want more than anything to help them in some way, as well as to use contemporary music to preach the gospel to the young people of Leningrad.

After a while he told me that his shift was over and that he had to take the ambulance back to the depot. He urged me to go with him, which I did. The depot was under a flyover. As we drove up to the complex and Valeri checked in, I thought to myself, 'Great, this is all Valeri needs to be questioned about a foreigner who doesn't speak a word of Russian sitting in his government vehicle.'

Valeri said to me, 'Don't talk, Tim, when others are around.' We pulled up in the yard where the vans are washed after every 24-hour shift. The lady doing the washing started to work on our van. Valeri leaned over to me and with a big grin said, 'I've been telling her about Jesus for several months: she's very interested and I think I'll talk to her again now.' With those words he climbed out of the van and started helping her with the washing. The whole time he was doing this he talked to her about the Lord. I couldn't understand exactly what he was saying, but his gestures expressed genuine warmth and caring for her. His smile was an expression of love. I could tell that this man loved to talk to others about 'his Jesus'.

Valeri hopped back in the van and drove it to another station to fill up the tank with petrol. A man came up to Valeri and they struck up a conversation. I tried to pretend I wasn't interested in what was going on so that I wouldn't get Valeri into trouble, but I think he sensed my uneasiness and leaned in to tell me, 'He's a brother'. We smiled at each other and acknowledged our common inheritance...without words.

At the final checkpoint a heavy-set man in his mid-fifties was sitting in a small cubicle-type office near the entrance. Valeri grabbed his time-log sheet and presented it to him. They exchanged a few words and we walked out of the garage. On the way out Valeri told me that he had witnessed to this man several times, but he wasn't interested. In fact, he said the man had reported Valeri to the depot manager and tried to get him dismissed for his religious activities. Apparently that had resulted in a job review and Valeri had been threatened with dismissal unless he stopped witnessing. His comment was: 'But Tim, how can I be a Christian and not witness about my Jesus?' I asked myself, 'Tim, do you have this kind of zeal? For you there are no risks for your family, job or livelihood, but see what they are for Valeri.'

We travelled a long distance by bus, stopped to buy a few things in a grocery shop and finally arrived back at the high-rise block I had visited the night before.

Valeri's wife, children and mother-in-law were all out. We sat in his living room and he began to share with me his musical ideas and dreams of recording and performing gospel rock music. He told me about the Christian rock musical that he had in his head for which he had begun to write out the lyrics. I explained a little about what I'd been doing in the Soviet Union, which made him very excited.

At that point he came over and sat next to me so we could talk in hushed tones. This is a standard precaution to prevent conversations from being picked up on surveillance equipment.

Valeri told me that he had a plan to escape from the Soviet Union with a friend. They wanted to go either to America or England and begin a gospel music group to record and produce good rock gospel music for the young people of the USSR. Then he said that he'd arranged with a Soviet sailor for him to be crated up in a shipment leaving for England the next day.

I was shocked. Immediately my thoughts turned to his wife and two small girls. I asked him, 'what about your wife and children, who'll take care of them?' Valeri answered with sincerity, 'the Lord will.' In my work with persecuted believers I'd heard this type of reasoning before and it's very difficult for a Westerner to judge. It seems that persecution over a long period of time can create a fatalistic or holy boldness (only the Lord knows which) in some Soviet citizens. Anyone facing the threat of a long prison term for his faith has to cope with being away from family and loved ones. I'm sure that Valeri tried to be realistic about his situation and decided that he would be away from his family whether he went to the West or whether he was eventually put in prison for his faith. He probably thought, 'why not go to the West? At least my time can be productive and maybe later I can get my wife and family out.'

The next question that raced through my mind was, 'How can Valeri know how difficult it is even for a Western gospel musician to accomplish what he wants to do, much less a Soviet émigré? All his life he has thought of the West as the land of golden opportunity; how can I explain to him that it isn't quite like that?'

I said to Valeri, 'It isn't easy to do all this, you know that, don't you?' His comment was quite logical, 'Easier than it is here! I just want to record my Christian musical.... In fact, I have ideas for two or three more in my head. There's nowhere for me to record here. It isn't sufficient to record on a stereo recorder, we need good equipment.'

My next words came involuntarily, yet I spoke to him with great conviction: 'Valeri, I've only known you for about an hour, but let me tell you as a brother in the Lord; this is a word from the Lord; he doesn't want you to leave the USSR tomorrow.' I was being very presumptuous. There I was, a Westerner who had nothing to lose either way, telling a persecuted believer not to flee to the West when he had the chance to do so.

Valeri's reply was astonishing. Smiling he said; 'This morning in my devotions the Lord told me that I would have the answer for which I've been praying the last three years: whether to leave the USSR for the West to carry out my recording and ministry plans or to stay put and wait for another direction. OK, it's decided, I won't go tomorrow.'

I then felt extremely humble that the Lord had used me to convey a message from him to Valeri who had been praying for guidance for so long.

Valeri asked me if I could help him to get access to musical and recording equipment, so that his music could be recorded and distributed among young people. I had earlier been instrumental in arranging for something similar for a group of young believers who had a similar vision to Valeri's.

I explained a little to him about these people, and told him to contact a certain individual and to share his ideas with him. I told Valeri that this person would help him if he was sure that this was part of God's will. Needless to say, Valeri was elated. Not only had the Lord provided him with an answer about leaving the country, but he had also opened a way for him to record a quality production of his music within the USSR, something he had never dreamed was possible.

By this time Valeri's wife, children and mother-in-law had returned and were carrying out their daily chores. We adjourned our meeting to the kitchen for some tea (served from an old silver samovar), black bread and cheese. Our conversation became more technical as we discussed how exactly he should proceed with his project. We talked about the necessity for Valeri to write down all his musical scores and lyrics on manuscript paper. We discussed which instruments he should use for the recording and how the project could be carried out.

By that time we had exhausted ourselves with conversation and Valeri asked me if there was anything I wanted to see in Leningrad and I requested a visit to

St Isaac's Cathedral. Valeri started for the bus stop, but I wasn't feeling up to an hour's bus ride into town, so I persuaded him to let me pay for a taxi. He stopped one and we jumped in. We conversed for a couple of minutes in English, but the whole time we were talking Valeri's eyes kept darting towards the driver. Finally he said to me, 'Tim, excuse me, I want to tell this driver about Jesus.' I sat back and watched as Valeri explained his faith to the taxi driver for thirty minutes. I followed their gestures carefully. Valeri's expressions were effervescent, overflowing with a sincere concern for the man. From the driver's reactions and expressions, I could tell he was interested. We finally arrived at the cathedral; I paid the driver and we got out. Apparently the man had listened eagerly to all Valeri had said and responded positively. Valeri had told him to pray for a Bible and to read it, so that through it the Lord would be able to reveal himself.

I thought to myself, 'If only we Westerners had this kind of zeal in sharing our faith. Valeri speaks even though this is a great personal risk. I must never take our freedoms and opportunities in the West for granted.' It is extraordinary to think that, in an age when we, in the USA, are deluged with the printed word, Christian enquirers in the USSR must be exhorted to pray to get their hands on a Bible.

After we had visited the cathedral it was time for me to return to the hotel to get ready for my flight to Moscow. We found another taxi, stopped near the hotel, paid the driver and stood on the pavement. We hugged each other and gave the traditional kiss on each cheek, to which by now I had grown accustomed. I set off along the pavement toward the hotel and turned for a last wave. Valeri waved back, grinning from ear to ear. I thought to myself, 'Valeri is truly a man close to God's heart.'

7: Trumpet Call to the Kremlin

God's intervention in Valeri's life through Tim pointed the way forward to a practical possibility of recording *The Trumpet Call*. Over the next couple of years he continued to work as a driver. Eventually he was dismissed from the ambulance service because of his open evangelism, but then managed to get work as a bus driver. In between shifts he devoted all his energy to music. When one of his workmates at the bus depot found out that Valeri was a Christian, he informed the boss and Valeri was again dismissed from his job. It became increasingly hard to find reasonably paid work and now Valeri had to take whatever was going. If you are out of work in the Soviet Union you can be charged with 'parasitism' and sentenced in the courts. He did manage to find the occasional job as a driver, which was what he liked best, but, as I mentioned in the previous chapter, he never complained, no matter how menial the tasks he had to perform.

What was most important was that he had found his sense of direction again and he devoted himself whole-heartedly to fulfilling his vision somehow to make a rock version of the gospel available to young people. He first had to form a new group. With the exception of Sergei Timokhin, bass guitarist, all the other members of Trumpet Call have remained anonymous. Valeri's only written comment in his account of this period is: 'The group was formed, I found the people, or rather God led me to the people, but I do not have the right to speak about them. . . .'

Valeri met Sergei in 1981 when he was looking for talented musicians to join his group. Sergei became a Christian through Valeri's witness and came to share many of his ideals. They became very close friends. After *The Trumpet Call* had been completed at the end of 1982 Valeri and Sergei recorded an interview on cassette which they sent to the West. The object of the interview was to explain the aims of the group and how the recording was made. As they had no real interviewer, they posed imaginary questions to each other in turn. In the first part they describe their musical tastes:

Question: What is your attitude to music?

Valeri: My attitude to music is one of love and respect. I like different kinds of music – classical, jazz. I enjoy disco music, but my favourite is hard rock, heavy metal. My favourite groups are the Beatles – they are the classics – Pink Floyd, Deep Purple and many others. It would be difficult to list them all. . . .

Sergei: As for me, I completely share Valeri's views on music and there's only one thing that I'd like to add. Music isn't the real foundation of our lives – for all our love of music it remains for us a form of self-expression, an attitude to life, but God is the corner-stone in our hearts and in our lives.

Valeri: I don't think it's just coincidence that Sergei and I came together in the same group. We have the same musical tastes, but we also share the same convictions. . . .

We know very little about Sergei's background. He was born in 1958 and as a teenager became a devoted rock music fan. I met him just once when I was in Leningrad in 1982. At that time his wife Nina had one baby, a boy named Andrei, but she has since had another child, a daughter named Masha. Sergei earned his living as a tailor, but like Valeri, he devoted much of his spare time to playing his guitar. I warmed to both Sergei and Nina immediately. Sergei struck me as a particularly friendly, open and serious-minded person. It was he who asked me questions about life in Britain – about the economy, strikes, unemployment, the political system and the situation in Northern Ireland. He told me he always listened to Western radio broadcasts and obviously he was anxious to keep himself well informed on current affairs. For such a tall, powerfully built man he had a surprisingly soft voice and gentle manner. His loyalty to Valeri was total and he demonstrated this on many occasions at great personal risk. Although they had such different personalities, they obviously worked well together as a team.

Having formed the group, they still had the most difficult task ahead. Valeri had access to studio equipment, but the recording had to be carried out in total secrecy. The group knew that they risked discovery by the KGB everytime they used the studio.

The recording equipment was carried back and forth, far away from Valeri's home. He was followed every time he left Leningrad and had to evade his 'companions' before he could meet up with the other members of the group. There were obviously enormous tensions because of these conditions, notwithstanding the prayer and commitment offered by all concerned. Any group of artists working together has disagreements and they have to work out their differences in order to produce a masterpiece. Even in ideal conditions there would inevitably have been clashes of personality, but these men and women were risking everything – their security, jobs, family life and freedom – by making the recording and one tiny mistake by any one of them could have resulted in the arrest of the whole group. For Valeri it was obviously a fraught time and he was not satisfied with the final recording from an artistic point of view. Given the conditions in which it was made, however, the fact that a recording even exists is a miracle. Valeri and Sergei described some of the practical difficulties they encountered with rehearsals and recording sessions:

> We had to rent or just beg premises, equipment and instruments. The musicians didn't know their instruments and all the equipment changed. . . . We constantly had to change the location of the recording. . . . We never managed to play through the whole work together as a group, it was just impossible. We recorded everything separately and when we had completed it the musicians said that if they had known what it was going to be like they would have had a completely different approach.

Valeri also revealed in a document he sent to Keston College in March 1983 that he had lost his voice during the recording of the Russian version.

> I had only a few hours for the vocals, so hoarseness or not, I still had to sing. . . .

What was Valeri like to work with? Did his 'holy boldness' frustrate or frighten the other members of the group? How did the other people involved arrange the practical side? The following extract from a letter written by one of the technicians involved in the recording conveys the atmosphere:

> During those nine months (1982) the recording took place in several different country cottages, and in two or three town apartments. It was hard work transporting all the equipment – sound insulation boards for the drums, food, personal belongings and people from place to place. Everything had to be planned in minute detail. We tried to be very careful not to be conspicuous to the neighbours. Depending on the location, the group had to stay inside the chosen building the whole time – they had little time for relaxation. Every time Valeri and Sergei came they were followed. But God

helped them to get rid of their 'tails' and they arrived safely. Valeri was told constantly not to go out, but sometimes he simply got fed up with his 'imprisonment' and went off. He always managed to bring back something to cheer us all up. God protected him and everybody else until finally the work was completed.

Unfortunately it is not possible to give further details of what actually happened during those months, because many of the people involved are still at liberty.

I should note here that when I was in Leningrad in 1982 I heard a cassette recording of the instrumental tracks from *The Trumpet Call*. As I listened to the music through headphones Valeri sang the lyrics and at the same time described and imitated all the special effects which he said would eventually be added when the group got the synthesiser (which I was asked to send in). From the beginning he had a very definite idea of what the finished work would sound like. He refused to allow anything to defeat him. The remarkable story of the synthesiser is a good example of how Valeri put all his trust in God and was categorical in his statements to other, less convinced members of the group that God would answer his prayer. I am grateful to my friend for telling his story in his own words:

I was carrying three large suitcases, two of them filled with tapes, clothes and medical items, the third with a standard synthesiser to be used for *The Trumpet Call* recording.

I approached the customs at Moscow airport, barely able to carry all the cases on my own. Of course I knew that there were many questions which I might be asked by the customs officials, but the most obvious one seemed to me to be why I was carrying so much luggage for a three-day visit! I watched the queue intently as a woman a few places in front of me had her bags turned inside out and even had to remove her jewellery so it could be declared properly. I prayed as I stumbled up to the counter. I was just about to load the cases onto the scan, as all passengers have to do at the airport customs, when one of the officials looked at the customs declaration form and said: 'You haven't filled this in correctly'. I thought, 'This is it, now I'll have to declare everything'. I had forgotten to write 'none' in the space for declaring jewellery and arms. I wrote it and apologised. He then said thank you and indicated that I could go on. I almost blurted out, 'but you haven't looked at my luggage'. I managed to stop myself, hurriedly picked up all the cases and walked to the main entrance where a taxi was waiting. As the taxi driver was loading everything into the boot he picked up the suitcase containing the synthesiser, groaned and said, 'What on earth have you got in here?' 'Oh, only a piano', I replied.

Later I walked around Moscow for a few hours praising God for such a miraculous touch. I had declared absolutely nothing and therefore would not have to bring anything back out of the country. (Normally you have to declare major items you bring in and take them out with you when you leave the country).

I took the train around midnight and travelled up to Leningrad. I arrived at the hotel early in the morning very tired, but I realised that I had no time to lose. However, after I had prayed, my intuition was not to go to Valeri's before midday, so I rested for a few hours.

I then gathered together as many items as possible – clothes, gifts and the synthesiser – and took a taxi, the underground and finally a bus, just to distract any interested followers. When I arrived at the flat no one was home except Zhanna and she had only come in for an hour between twelve and one p.m. Characteristically, she did her best to talk to me in broken English, smiling all the time. I deposited all the goods and stayed for a while. Zhanna told me to come back at six o'clock, so

I left, visited other contacts and made my way back just after six.

Valeri had been praying and had told the other members of the band (in particular the keyboard player) that the synthesiser would be provided before they left to start the recording (which was to be the evening of the following day). In England we had known nothing about the time of starting the recording, but God had coordinated everything. Valeri was so moved and overjoyed that he went out straight away to phone the keyboard player who reacted with total disbelief. Valeri had to spend several minutes trying to convince him that the synth. had actually arrived. Within twenty minutes he was round at Valeri's flat looking absolutely stunned. He was not yet a fully convinced believer, but God was certainly demonstrating his power to this young man.

I spent the rest of the evening chatting to Valeri and his family, talking about everything from the second coming of Christ to the latest pop scene. His record collection amazed me, everything from Cliff Richard to 2nd Chapter of Acts (a Christian group) and many others, both Christian and secular. He was also interested to know which famous artists had become Christians – like Bob Dylan whose records he had. He always listened to Western radio broadcasts and tried to glean as much information as he could about the music scene in Britain and America. Apart from anything else, this provided a very natural talking point in his contacts with Leningrad youth. I left late at night, tired, but rejoicing for such a loving and zealous brother in Christ.

I spent the whole of the next day with Valeri and we visited the home of the keyboard player and sang songs (including a few old Beatles numbers) with him and his fiancée, who was one of the backing vocalists in the group. They had so little equipment that we had to play the synthesiser through the TV in order to amplify it. We had a wonderful time of prayer together and then Valeri and I left in order to visit a young woman who worked in a local café who had agreed to travel with the group and cook for them while they were recording. She was a radiant Christian who had a great zeal to serve God, even though her circumstances were not easy. The café where she worked was frequented by army and police officials because her cooking had earned such a good reputation.

We talked almost non-stop that day while visiting what seemed like the whole of Leningrad. Valeri is a man who is always seeking to serve God and love his neighbour. We visited the Leningrad Baptist Church where about forty people were being baptised that day. The church was so full that we could not even squeeze inside to stand in the aisle at the back. But even in the church there were some officials who were not in the least bit interested in the things of God – they were acting as 'watch-dogs' for the KGB. Despite the fact that many of his friends had been interrogated by these informers, Valeri always said, 'God is their judge'.

Valeri is a visionary, wanting to use any means possible to tell people about Jesus, whether through music or just by letting his workmates know how God has so radically changed his life. We parted on Sunday night. He was going off to do the recording and I, unfortunately, had to return to Moscow and then to London.

Having completed the recording, Valeri wanted it to be heard – not just in the Soviet Union, but throughout the world. He knew that the most difficult period of his ministry lay ahead. It is significant that for Valeri, one of the most important preparations for the coming battle concerned the spiritual well-being of his wife and daughters. It was as if Valeri knew that a time would come when they would have to stand on their own without him and only a strong faith would carry them through.

I knew that when we had finished the recording there would be a battle. More than anything I wanted my family to be a believing one, to be a completely Christian family – just as the church is a family. I asked the girls, 'Do you want to be baptised?' Previously they had told me that they would like to be baptised, but this time I asked them concretely, 'Do you want to go and be baptised?' 'Yes, we do!' 'Are you sure you want to do this, for your own sakes?' 'Yes, for our sakes.' So the children were baptised.

Because of the difficulty in the Baptist Church for any child under eighteen to be baptised, Zhanna and Marina were baptised in an Orthodox Church. This was later cited as one of the reasons for expelling Valeri from the Baptist Church. Valeri continued:

Tanya had already been baptised as a child, but she agreed to be 'confirmed'.* After taking this step she became a witness too, even at work. Somehow she became bolder – before that she had never witnessed to her faith.

During December 1982 Valeri and Sergei fasted and prayed together before taking an unprecedented step. Their ambition was boundless and even now it is difficult to believe that they really expected to achieve what they set out to do. They wrote to the Presidium of the Supreme Soviet of the USSR about their rock musical. They obviously decided that to try by legal means to get it performed publicly would be to their advantage and they probably hoped that it would also help to make their names known in the West. On 17th January they wrote and signed an

* It is not clear from the Russian text what Valeri means here as neither the Baptists nor the Russian Orthodox practice confirmation as such.

'Open Appeal' addressed to the Presidium of the Supreme Soviet of the USSR. Carbon copies were designated for Keston College, the United Nations Organisation, Christian leaders of the world and concerned international organisations. The appeal read as follows:

To the Presidium of the Supreme Soviet of the USSR
We, the members of a Leningrad Christian musical group, Trumpet Call, which was organised before the face of Almighty God and by his will, call upon you to grant us permission to stage open performances of religious music in the concert halls of our country.

Our repertoire is of a purely religious nature and has no relation to political or anti-state activity.

Our aim is to open the path to the highest values for all men, to serve the well-being of the people and to seek eternal life through salvation in Jesus Christ, the Son of God. Everyone who comes to faith in Christ becomes a worthy member of society, and our country stands in particular need of such people.

Although we recorded our rock opera unofficially in order to avoid the possibility of unconstitutional persecution, we cannot think that you are opposed to believers generally, and our group in particular, as we stand for love, justice and peace throughout the world.

We are sending this appeal by post, but in order to ensure that it does reach you, we have decided to make it public.

With respect,

Signed: Valeri Barinov (address)
        Sergei Timokhin (address)

17th January 1983

Valeri and Sergei took this appeal to the post office in the form of a registered letter, and there it was subsequently confiscated by the local authorities. As soon as the two men realised what had happened, they decided to go to Moscow in person to deliver the appeal and distribute some copies of the cassette recording of *The Trumpet Call*. On 24th January the appeals were retyped and Valeri and Sergei boarded the night train to Moscow. The events that followed gave rise to a subsequent communication with the Presidium. This one, dated 25th January, was entitled 'Declaration' and signed by Valeri. The text read:

Please be advised that on 24th January 1983, I, Valeri Alexandrovich Barinov, and my friend Sergei Timokhin had intended to travel to Moscow on the night train.

For no apparent reason, we were arrested at 11.20 p.m. and taken to the militia room at Leningrad's Moscow Station. No reason was given for this illegal arrest. On the contrary, my friend was ordered to empty his pockets and then subjected to a body search. My pockets were emptied by a militiaman. The operation was directed by a man in plain clothes, who did not identify himself at any point. Two witnesses were present as well as about ten militiamen.

The plain-clothes man, presumably a KGB official, subjected us to a stream of verbal abuse and held us until 2 a.m. He stated that he would be speaking to us 'in a different vein' in a couple of days' time. When we were finally turned out, he warned us not to leave Leningrad, and confiscated ten letters and three cassettes from our belongings.

Signed: Valeri Barinov.

A handwritten note was attached requesting that copies be forwarded to a number of Christian organisations and individuals, including Dr Billy Graham.

Despite this setback, Valeri and Sergei managed to find someone to take the appeals to Moscow three days later. Valeri's interpretation of these events was that the Leningrad KGB did not want Moscow to hear about the existence of *The Trumpet Call* and decided to deal swiftly with the issue themselves. In subsequent letters to organisations and individuals in the West, Valeri gave a full account of what followed. All these direct quotations are taken from two letters written in March and June 1983, the latter addressed to President Reagan:

On 28th January I was summoned by the local official from the Council for Religious Affairs (CRA) in Leningrad, Nikolai Nikolaevich Kirov. He said, quoting the Constitution of the USSR, that the authorities would not give permission for the group to perform publicly. He added that communists should be waging an ideological war against religion. A KGB officer who was present during the conversation said, 'I like your music, but if you want us to help you, don't sing about God'.

In the next interview with Valeri and Sergei a more threatening tone was adopted.

Then we had another meeting with a different KGB official – the one who had detained us at the Moscow Station on 24th January. This was in the presence of the CRA official, Kirov, who tried to intimidate us, saying that we would be treated as dissidents, taken from Leningrad to beyond the Ural mountains and that our children and our wives would become the most wretched of people.

Although they received no official acknowledgement or any written reply to their appeal, the official attitude had been made clear and Valeri and Sergei had received their first warning. But events were to take a more sinister turn.

The day before his first interview with Kirov at the CRA Valeri had had an unexpected and unwelcome visitor.

On 27th January a lieutenant in uniform came to my flat. He was a district militiaman. He told me to go, as a matter of urgency, to the military commission, although I had received no notification about this. I went to the commission in the Vyborg district and was told that they intended to call me up to do two months' military service. Then I was sent for a medical examination.

Valeri had, of course, completed his two years' compulsory conscription twenty years earlier, but was still on the list of reservists. In the event, this call-up was simply a pretext for a campaign of harassment against him. He continued:

The KGB used this cunning device to hand me over to a psychiatrist and a nerve specialist and they, in turn sent me on to the psycho-neurological clinic (PND). (PND is the Russian abbreviation for psycho-neurological clinic). The commission's psychiatrist and nerve specialist, after talking to me for one and a half hours, did not want to have anything to do with me and referred me to the psychiatric centre at the Skvortsov Stepanov hospital in the Vyborg district.

Valeri was told by this specialist that if he witnessed to his faith in the army he would end up in a psychiatric ward. He gave Valeri a referral notice which stated that he saw himself as playing a role in God's providence, that he spoke about the power of Christ and actively preached divine wisdom, and so on.

I sent the notice of referral to the West [now in Keston College archive] because in such circumstances one must establish each step one takes. At the clinic I handed over another paper which the military authorities had given me when I attended the medical commission. It was signed by all the doctors and the psychiatrist had written on it 'referred to the psycho-neurological clinic (PND)'. At the psychiatric clinic I saw the duty doctor, Maslova, and had a good conversation with her. She was on the point of confirming that I was absolutely sane, but was suddenly deterred when I mentioned the fact that our group had received 'international support'.* 'Wait a minute in the corridor, I can't decide this alone', she said. I was left alone for about an hour. I was then invited into another room, No. 60, where three doctors and Maslova were waiting for me. There I spent about five minutes, but no real conversation was possible because they treated me as if I was an absolute idiot. However this act did not upset me too much. In the end the one who was evidently the head doctor said to me, 'Valeri, you need not report again to the military authorities. We've decided that you must undergo psychiatric investigation, so just wait'. I asked what I must wait for. 'Just wait and don't worry', Maslova replied. 'You'll soon understand everything'. I went home, but I did manage to leave a copy of our cassette for them which they listened to and, apparently, liked. The cassette was my only defence against being put away by the psychiatrists in some place where even international support would not help.

Valeri tried to retain the initiative by giving a copy of the tape to his interrogators. He would never miss an opportunity to convert even the KGB. But Valeri was right to fear the consequences of compulsory confinement in a psychiatric hospital. Despite an international outcry against the practice of confining sane people in mental

---

* Valeri was probably referring to the fact that by now his appeal had been mentioned on the BBC Russian Service.

institutions, there are still many victims of psychiatric abuse in the Soviet Union today.

There was no relief from the pressure at home, either. Throughout February Valeri's flat was under constant KGB surveillance. Members of the family were followed each time any of them left the flat. The girls were even followed to school. Despite this blatant harassment, Valeri retained his sense of humour and decided to have some fun with his watch dogs.

During February the occupants of Building 24, Block 3 on the Severny Prospekt witnessed the way in which the KGB were keeping me under surveillance. They noticed that a car was permanently stationed near the dustbins, next to the metal garages and that these cars were constantly changed. As a rule, there were two or more passengers in each car. When I informed a few of the occupants of the block about this, the cars disappeared. We decided to carry out a little experiment. They watched and I went out of the entrance of their block and walked up to the parked car. When I was only a few metres away from it, the car drove off immediately with all its occupants. During an interval of 20 minutes I approached the parked car five times, and each time the car moved off and was replaced by another. When the KGB agents realised they were the object of an experiment, they disappeared.

The KGB agents may have disappeared on that occasion, but not for long. In March Valeri received another visit from the local militiaman.

Yesterday evening* I was paid a visit by a local militiaman. It was the same one who, about two months ago, invited me (if you can call it that) to present myself to the military authorities (although I had received no official notification to do so). This time he gave me two

* Undated letter written in early March 1983.

options – either he would take me in a police car to spend the night feeding bed bugs in a preliminary investigation cell, from which I would be taken next morning to a compulsory investigation in a psychiatric hospital, or I could report there voluntarily at 10 a.m. the next day. Of course I didn't want to spend the night in a cell, so I gave him to understand that I would go voluntarily in the morning; However, the next morning, convinced of my perfect state of health, I decided there was no need to subject myself to a compulsory psychiatric examination. Experience is a great teacher. Trusting in the Lord, I had written my appeal not only to the Supreme Soviet of the USSR, but also to international organisations. Although there has been no reply from the Supreme Soviet, international public opinion has already heard of our plight through the BBC and through the Western press. Therefore instead of reporting to the psychiatric hospital I went away. As I write this letter, I'm conscious of how good it is to live with God who gives us patience in such circumstances. . . .

It is interesting to note that from the moment Valeri decided to 'go public', for him the most significant factor in retaining his liberty, apart from God's grace, was Western reaction and world public opinion. His faith in the ability of the latter to influence the Soviet authorities in their dealings with 'dissidents' places a great responsibility on Christians who live in free societies. He has always believed firmly that the Soviet authorities would think twice before committing violations of human rights if there were sufficient publicity abroad. In the West this is treated as a contentious issue, though the support for it is virtually universal among those who are persecuted in the USSR.

As has also happened with others, no immediate action was taken after Valeri failed to turn up at the psychiatric hospital, but the medical authorities still decided to register Valeri as a psychiatric patient. This meant that they were empowered to detain him at any time or place, incarcerate him in a mental hospital without examination and keep him there for as long as they wished. This was the threat that hung over Valeri and his family for many months until finally it became reality and he later found himself in the hands of white-coated KGB agents brandishing hypodermic needles. Meanwhile Tanya and Sergei, infuriated by the latest intimidatory tactic, sprang to Valeri's defence. Tanya went to the hospital. Valeri described the event as follows:

On 13th April I learned from nurse Yudina, who visited me from the PND attached to the Skvortsov Stepanov hospital, that they had placed me on the register of psychiatric patients without my knowledge. What is astonishing about this whole farce organised by representatives of the local authorities is that people working in a humanitarian profession agreed to take part. These are people including the doctors Maslova and Podsuk, who are bound by the Hippocratic oath. When my wife went to see Doctor Podsuk in order to find out why they had placed me on the register, she simply avoided the question and tried to remain silent. When Tanya insisted that she wanted to know the diagnosis, Podsuk replied that she did not have the right to give any information because the diagnosis was a professional secret. The other doctor, Maslova, avoided speaking about this subject to my wife in just the same way.

Sergei acted very boldly, ignoring the possible consequences to himself and demonstrating great loyalty to Valeri. On 21st April he wrote an 'Appeal' addressed to 'Christians, Christian organisations and world public opinion' and sent it abroad:

I, Sergei Timokhin, a member of the Christian group the Trumpet Call, want to make known to world public opinion the fact that on 13th April 1983 the nurse

Yudina, from the psycho-neurological clinic in the Vyborg district of Leningrad, made known the fact that my friend – the leader of our rock group, Valeri Barinov – has been placed on the register of psychiatric patients without his knowledge. This means that he is now registered as sick and is not therefore regarded as a fully responsible citizen. His closest relatives were not informed about the diagnosis and were told that it constituted a professional secret. One should point out that the doctors insisted more than once on a medical examination and for this they resorted to threats issued by the militia.

I, for my part, protest most strongly against the registration of Barinov as a psychiatric patient. I am his friend and collaborator and have been involved in Christian work with him for several years. I consider him completely normal. Our musical work with lyrics, music and arrangements written by Valeri is evidence of this fact, as is his organisational skill in arranging the recording in the most difficult circumstances – in a country where atheism prevails.

We openly sent an appeal to the Presidium of the Supreme Soviet of the USSR requesting permission to perform our Christian musical publicly and in connection with this we were told in the presence of an official from the Council for Religious Affairs, Nikolai Nikolaevich Kirov, by a KGB officer who was attempting to frighten us that we would be classed as dissidents. We see, on the basis of many facts already mentioned, that his words are not far from reality.

We expect and fear new repression and provocation from the authorities and I therefore appeal to world public opinion to defend us and our families. Raise your voices in defence of our Christian group the Trumpet Call and all believers – we beg you to pray for us. And we believe that God, in his power, will complete his work through us his feeble servants. For the Lord said: 'Trust in me – do not be ashamed'.

21st April 1983

Sergei Timokhin

One consequence of Valeri's new-found status as a mental patient was the loss of his job. As he was no longer 'responsible' for his actions he was not allowed to continue as a chauffeur. Tanya had found it virtually impossible to get any information from doctors Maslova and Podsuk, but the one thing they did tell her to do was to warn Valeri not to apply for any job which involved driving. He was dismissed from his job as a driver a few weeks later on 13th May. Tanya became the only breadwinner and it was virtually impossible to manage on her meagre salary. Two days after the visit from Nurse Yudina, Valeri was again summoned to the CRA. During the interview he was given a strong hint that a case was being prepared against him for alleged slander against the Soviet State and social system. It should be noted that during all the interviews with KGB personnel, psychiatrists or CRA officials Valeri was closely questioned about Western visitors and the authorities made no secret of the fact that they strongly disapproved of his contact with 'agents of Western imperialism'. Once again the family home came under siege. At that time there were often as many as ten different cars, each with three occupants, stationed around the block of flats.

At the same time as all these pressures were mounting Valeri was experiencing great spiritual blessing. By this time many more Christians from all over the Soviet Union had heard about the group and what Valeri was trying to achieve and a 'chain of prayer' had started to operate on his behalf. Apart from the tapes of *The Trumpet Call* which were circulating among young people in Leningrad, copies in Russian and English had reached the West. On 11th and 12th March Seva Novgorodtsev who was the DJ for the BBC Russian Service pop programme, read out the full text of Valeri's 'Open appeal' and 'Declaration' over the air and played some extracts from the Russian version of *The Trumpet Call*. He also read out the home addresses of both Valeri and Sergei and fan mail started pouring in to Leningrad from all over the Soviet Union. A sample of these remarkable letters eventually reached Keston College. Valeri and Sergei started corresponding personally with many of the letter writers. The response they received from a wide cross section of people, mainly in the 15 – 30 age range, gave them tremendous hope. Valeri wrote:

Sergei and I have received many letters from different parts of the country which express support for our sincere aims and condemnation of the unlawful activities carried out by the authorities. On the basis of these letters it's evident that people, and especially young people, are beginning to wake up from a spiritual slumber which has been brought about by atheism. People are beginning to understand that a desolate soul cannot be satisfied with alcohol, drugs or even with wealth. And in these letters, it is as if the cry of the spirit of our people is expressed – we want to know about God, we need God, we are tired of the atheist brochures which are lying about on the shelves of our bookshops, we want the Bible, which even the majority of believers have never seen.

In response specifically to these letters, Valeri wrote a detailed reply addressed to all the listeners to *The Trumpet Call*. He gave an account of the difficulties he had been facing, together with information about the Trumpet Call group and its aims, and sent it to Seva with the request that it be broadcast over Western radio to the Soviet Union. This happened on 30th April. As a result a second batch of letters from people who had heard this broadcast arrived at the homes of Valeri and Sergei.

A few months later, in July, there was a remarkable

follow-up to Seva's broadcasts. Cliff Richard's example had sparked Valeri into creativity and it therefore came as a tremendous encouragement when Cliff recorded a short statement commenting on *The Trumpet Call* which was broadcast by the BBC Russian Service. The following is an extract from what Cliff said:

Recently I heard a tape by a group from the Soviet Union called the Trumpet Call and they play really fine rock'n'roll.... I know that the Soviet Union hasn't had rock'n'roll in its culture and so it's a great thrill to find that there is a band which enjoys the kind of music I like and which is really playing it well. But even more than that, the joy for me is that this band is a Christian one and that in the words of their songs they are presenting God and their faith in Jesus. I find that very exciting because when I first became a Christian I was told by everybody: 'No, it's impossible, you cannot be a Christian and sing rock'n'roll'.

You see, I'm not a painter or a writer or a great actor, but I can sing and so my only way of communicating, my only art, is my music and the words of my songs. And so for eighteen years now I've been presenting Jesus in much of my music and I know it can work. And so I just want to encourage you to listen to bands like the Trumpet Call, and I want to encourage the Trumpet Call, too. There may be opposition from within your churches, even to the point of saying, 'No, it's not God's music', but *you* are God's people and God uses people. If you can sing rock'n'roll then you should sing it and present Jesus as best you can and I believe that it will bring glory to God.

The intense interest expressed by young people in this new phenomenon – a real, live Christian rock group – gave Valeri and Sergei new opportunities for evangelism on an unprecedented scale. However, they did not receive support or encouragement from the church. On the contrary, there was opposition. The church leaders were obviously alarmed by this influx of unconverted youth and simply did not know how to deal with the situation. The following letter, dated 6th March 1983 and addressed to the Leningrad Council of Evangelical Christians and Baptists, was a genuine attempt on the part of Valeri and Sergei to be reconciled with those in authority:

'Blessed are the people who know the festal shout, who walk, O Lord, in the light of thy countenance' (Psalm 89.15★).

Dear brothers and sisters in Christ Jesus our Lord.

With deep love and respect, we, Valeri Barinov and Sergei Timokhin, in the name of the Trumpet Call group and before the face of Almighty God, address you in order to put before you the true aim of our work and to explain the path on which the Lord has set us.

Recently in all churches there has been preaching about the imminent coming of our Lord Jesus Christ and about God's trumpet. And out of his great love and mercy to sinners and to his bride, the church, the Lord has already begun to sound his trumpet through us, his weak and unworthy servants. The form of the preaching of the Trumpet Call group may seem strange to you, but thanks to the medium of modern music God's word is made accessible to everybody and, most importantly, to young people. Therefore the aim of our work is to witness to his glorious coming. And we are addressing you with a request: to understand that we are fellow workers in God's harvest field and not to place obstacles in our way as happened on 9th February this year.

We want to inform you that we invited to the Leningrad

★ In the Russian version of the Bible the words *trubny zov* (trumpet call) appear instead of 'festal shout'.

Evangelical Christian-Baptist prayer house those who had expressed an interest in our Christian music outreach in order to witness to them about God and the purpose of our group and to play a recording of our music. On 6th February we alerted the elders to this invitation, which was planned for a day when there was no service, but after a choir practice. At 9 p.m. on 9th February about 30 to 40 people gathered at the prayer house, but Alexander Semyonovich Morozov, (Chairman of the Leningrad Church Council) who came out to meet those who had gathered, forbade what had been arranged. Later we learned that a further 200 people arrived that evening. And so we beg you not only not to place obstacles in our way, but to support us in our aims and to pray that Almighty God will give the opportunity to preach openly about the coming Christ.

We thank our God that he has set us apart for this ministry and believe that placing our hope in him we will not be put to shame.

Valeri Barinov
Sergei Timokhin

Such opportunities for evangelism among the city drop-outs were unique. The church leadership could not possibly deny that Valeri's ministry was bearing fruit. But they were faced with a dilemma. They did not officially approve of his methods of evangelism, but how could they ignore the needs of the young people who were coming to church directly as a result of Valeri's influence? Sadly, they chose to ignore the evidence that God was powerfully working in their midst and, under pressure from the KGB, started a slander campaign against Valeri. In March 1983 I had the opportunity, with Mike Rowe of Keston College, to meet the newly appointed General Secretary of the Baptist Union, Bernard Green, prior to his first visit to Moscow in that capacity. He received us at our request because we wanted him to raise Valeri's case with the Baptist leadership in Moscow. By this time the *Baptist Times* in the UK had carried two front-page articles about Valeri, 'Tell the world about our plea' on 24th February and 'Army for you' on 3rd March. We asked Bernard Green to express the concern felt by British Christians, and particularly Baptists, about the way Valeri was being harassed by the authorities. Mr Green carried out our request. Unfortunately he was not able to meet Valeri personally. When he returned to the UK he telephoned me and reported what the Moscow leadership had had to say about Valeri. It made painful hearing. It amounted to the allegation that Valeri was a drunkard and a womaniser who mixed with unsavoury company.

Unfortunately church leaders of all denominations in the Soviet Union have too often been willing to collaborate with the KGB and help them to defame people. The victims have no opportunity to defend themselves, no right of reply to articles published in the Soviet press. In the First Epistle to the Corinthians, Paul addresses the Christians at Corinth as 'babes in Christ'. He warns them not to think of themselves as wise, as having learnt all that is required about living the Christian life. He then compares his own reputation in society, his sufferings and those of other apostles, with the apparently easy life of the Corinthian Christians. The following verses are relevant to the situation in the Soviet Union where many Christians are reviled for their faith and perhaps we, in Western societies are the 'babes in Christ; as well as those church leaders in the Soviet Union who receive privileges and concessions from the Soviet state in return for compromise. Paul says:

> We are fools for Christ's sake, but you are wise in Christ. We are weak, but you are strong. You are held in honour, but we are in disrepute. To the present hour we hunger and thirst, we are ill-clad and buffeted and homeless, and we labour, working with our own hands. When reviled, we bless; when persecuted, we endure;

when slandered, we try to conciliate; we have become, and are now, as the refuse of the world, the offscouring of all things (1 Cor. 4.10–13, RSV).

One does not know what pressure is exerted on the church leaders to make them comply. They too pay a heavy penalty, because they must live with their consciences.

On 29th June a formal decision was taken by members of the Leningrad Church to expel Valeri from the congregation. In fact he had known about this decision since April, but had continued to attend the church as if nothing had happened. He wrote about this in a letter addressed to my husband, Michael, dated 7th July 1983.

Greetings to you Michael and to all our friends.

I want to inform you that on 29th June 1983 at a members' meeting I was expelled from the church. On 28th June I was in church and wanted to discuss this matter with the elders in the presence of my group. I took with me all the letters sent to Sergei and me by admirers of *The Trumpet Call*. The conversation didn't get us anywhere. They wouldn't read the letters. They were not cold towards me, but very cautious. I felt that they were under great pressure from the KGB. It was clear to me that it would be pointless to go to the members' meeting and that the decision dictated by the KGB would be carried out – to expel me from the Baptist Church. Friends told me later that they had expelled me for the following reasons:

– my appearance: I wear jeans and a cross;
– my children have been baptised in the Orthodox Church on the basis of their own faith and insistence, because in the Baptist Church you are not allowed to be baptised until the age of 18;
– because of our Christian rock group, the Trumpet

Call, which has been partly responsible for a spiritual awakening among young people in our country;
– because I do not call myself a Baptist, but a Christian.

In other words, they expelled me for disobeying the elders. But the Lord is our shepherd. I think that the aim of a pastor should be to teach others how to be close to God – how God leads his sheep is his concern.

I want to point out that I don't have any enemies at all, not even in my own church. I have a peaceful and loving attitude towards all fellow believers and if some or the elders don't understand me, then I can accept that and I love them with all the love of Christ.

Of course, it was very unpleasant for me to hear that I had been expelled from my own church, but I thank God for it, knowing that it's part of my journey in life, my cross. And my only desire is to fulfil his holy will, not my own will or the will of my fellow men. What is important is not how I'm judged by others, but how I'm judged by God. Our Lord Jesus Christ will be glorified. With his body he takes away all our weakness and with his blood he washes away all our sins. Whoever believes in the sacrifice of Christ, whether he's a weak Christian or a strong one, will not be judged by God, far less by men. And during these last days before Christ returns, every Christian, especially in our atheist country, ought to live according to the principle established by Jesus Christ in Matt. 16.25: 'For whoever would save his life will lose it, and whoever loses his life for my sake will find it.'

On 22nd June a psychiatrist visited me. He asked about my health. I replied that it was fine and that I considered myself to be completely healthy. I asked him on what basis I'd been registered as a psychiatric patient without a statutory examination. I told him that this was illegal. But immediately he interrupted me and said that he knew nothing about me, that he'd come to see me on the request of the head doctor at the PND. He added that I ought to talk to this head doctor. Then I told him that I wasn't allowed to do the kind of work I was qualified to do (as a driver) because of being registered as a psychiatric patient. He immediately said goodbye and left. However, I managed to say to him that I was completely healthy and that I wasn't going to the PND. I know that the aim of the KGB is to get rid of me by handing me over to the psychiatrists.

On 25th June a local policeman came to see me. I wasn't at home and he talked to my daughter, Zhanna. He wanted to know how long I'd been out of work and why I was not working. Zhanna answered that I had been dismissed on 13th May. As he was leaving he asked her to tell me to go to see him. Of course I didn't go.

Thank God, many believers realise that I was expelled from the church by the KGB. With regard to this there's one interesting fact: the elders know that I've been registered as a psychiatric patient and, as a rule, they do not expel such believers, because they feel compassion towards them and realise that they are sick. One has to ask the question – why did they expel me? . . .

Greetings from us to everyone. The most important thing is that we should pray that God will fulfil his purpose through us. Eternal praise to our all-powerful God. He is the same, yesterday, today and forever. He does great miracles through his weak, but chosen servants. With respect and love to you all, our dear friends.

Valeri   7th July 1983.

Do not fear for us, we are in the hands of Jesus. Amen.

Valeri simply refused to accept the decision made by the church leaders and would not allow himself to be excluded from the life of the church, even though he was no longer permitted to take communion. On the very day that he heard the outcome of the members' meeting (29th June) he and Sergei had just started a week of fasting and prayer in preparation for a big evangelistic meeting which they planned to hold at the Baptist church on 10th July. They sent word to Christian friends in the West about this meeting asking them to publicise it and to join in prayer for the event. This is a quotation from a telex sent out by Keston College on 28th June:

> Keston College has just received the latest in a series of appeals from Christian rock musicians, Valeri Barinov and Sergei Timokhin, in Leningrad. On Sunday 10th July they have decided to stage an unofficial performance of Christian rock music with young people having been invited to come to the Leningrad Baptist Church. Barinov and Timokhin are starting a week of prayer and fasting today in preparation for this event. They ask Western Christians to join them in prayer and for Western agencies to publicise the fact that the meeting will be taking place.

No detailed information was received concerning this event, except that Anatoli Morozov refused to allow the young people who came to enter the church.

Spurred on by the wonderful response he had had to *The Trumpet Call*, Valeri, while he was out of work, decided to concentrate on writing a second rock musical. He already had many ideas in his head and one story that he had always intended to use as a basis for a new work was that of blind Bartimaeus found in Mark's Gospel. Valeri felt an affinity with Bartimaeus because he had himself been spiritually blind and Jesus had made him see. However, this proved impossible. The KGB presence everywhere paralysed his creativity. He also knew that he would have to find another job very quickly or a charge would be brought against him. Already in his letter to Michael of 7th July he had asked about the possibility of receiving an invitation to work in Britain on his next rock musical. At the same time he was actively seeking contact with foreigners in Leningrad. In July he met a group of American students. One of them, John, wrote about their encounter with Valeri as follows:

The way in which we met Valeri was very interesting. We were all members of a group of 130 students from the Council for International Educational Exchange and were staying for one and a half months at Leningrad University. Valeri approached 'A' in a museum and told him he was 'looking for Christians'. The Lord answered his prayers and we both gained much from each other over the course of the following weeks.

Valeri was always happiest when in the company of Christians from abroad. He was then able completely to put aside the depressing reality of his life in Leningrad with all its pressures and problems and project himself into a new situation. Before long, wearing his 'I love NY' T-shirt, he was experiencing in his own imagination life in Britain or America with his Western friends. It was often very difficult for his foreign visitors to bring Valeri down to earth. I have heard more than one person say, after visiting him, 'Well, when you're with Valeri, no matter how preposterous his ideas are, he has such faith in God that you end up believing anything is possible'.

It came as no surprise to me to hear from John that Valeri was once again trying to think of ways to escape from the USSR. His latest plan was to try a 'passport switch'. His idea was that someone from the West should enter the USSR, arrange a secret meeting with Valeri, hand over his passport which would then presumably be forged with Valeri's photo, signature and details and later, after Valeri had left the country, the Westerner would report to his Consulate that the passport had been stolen. My immediate reaction to this suggestion was, 'How could

Valeri possibly imagine that such a crazy idea would work?' But how can one expect people, when they have never had the chance to travel abroad, to know about the precise nature of passport regulations? Not surprisingly, nothing ever came of this idea.

Valeri was able to take a short holiday in August with Tanya and the two girls. When he arrived back in Leningrad in September he managed to get a job in a local park, hosing water on a large expanse of concrete to create a skating rink. No doubt he was mentally composing a future rock opera while he performed this exceedingly boring mechanical task.

During the first half of 1983 we had become accustomed to receiving telephone calls at our house from Valeri. There are many Christians in the Soviet Union who try to keep up their friendships with people in the West by phoning, but of course they know that every word they say is noted by the authorities. Valeri often used to phone early in the morning and these brief conversations were always an absolute delight. Valeri was invariably full of life and joy talking about his Lord. We exchanged greetings and bits of family news and assured each other of mutual prayer support. However, I always had a dread of hearing about the next move in the KGB plan to make life difficult for Valeri and his family.

One evening in October the phone rang at about eleven thirty p.m. I picked up the receiver, but after a series of clicks the line went dead. An instinct told me that this was someone trying to call from the Soviet Union. Why so late? What can have happened? When the phone rang about 45 minutes later the Leningrad operator came on the line. Michael picked up one receiver and I the other and with great anxiety we waited for Valeri to come on the line. 'Hello, Hello, Michael, is that you? It's Sergei here. Valeri has just been arrested. Yes, they've taken him to psychiatric hospital.'

I listened with disbelief as Sergei revealed in a calm, steady voice the details of what had happened and asked us to do all we could to publicise the event. That night we interceded for Valeri as never before.

There were two major events within two days at which we were able to announce what had happened and urge people to pray. One was the Keston College Open Day with over 200 people present. During the afternoon we kept a minute's silence to remember Valeri and his family. The other event was an evangelistic rally in Blackheath near London attended by well over a thousand young people. Prayers were offered publicly for Valeri by the evangelist, Eric Delve, who was speaking on that occasion. We learned later that at the same time some members of the Leningrad Church had also prayed earnestly for Valeri.

As well as prayer there was publicity. News of Valeri's detention was announced on Western radio stations broadcasting in Russian to the USSR. The story was taken up widely by the British and overseas press, both church and secular.

On 18th October Sergei wrote a bold appeal on behalf of all the members of the Trumpet Call group to the Presidium of the Supreme Soviet demanding that Valeri be released immediately from psychiatric hospital. His appeal reveals many details about the actual conditions under which Valeri was detained.

I, Sergei Timokhin, appeal to you on behalf of the Christian musical group, the Trumpet Call.

In the name of the other members of this group I wish to lodge a strong protest against the incarceration of the founder of our group, Valeri Barinov, in psychiatric hospital. This illegal act was perpetrated on 11th October 1983 at 1 p.m. in the Leningrad underground station Udelnaya where Barinov was detained by the militia and subsequently delivered to Leningrad Psychiatric Hospital No. 3 (the Skvortsov Stepanov Hospital).

There is reason to fear that Barinov, whom they allege

to be ill, will be subjected to enforced psychiatric treatment under the guise of psychiatric testing of his mental state. These fears are not ungrounded, for Barinov was given injections of the strong neuroleptic, aminazin, from the day of his admission into the hospital.

Literally hundreds of people, including Barinov's close friends, relatives and workmates, could testify that he is in sound mental health and is absolutely normal.

To thrust a mentally healthy person into a psychiatric hospital with the genuinely insane is an inhuman act in itself. When, as in Barinov's case, this is further supplemented by forced injection of neuroleptics, by round the clock confinement within four walls, by forbidding him to read or write or to receive letters, by forbidding him to approach a window and, finally, by refusing to permit visits from his closest friends and relatives (with the sole exception of his wife) – then such a stay in the psychiatric hospital is truly soul-destroying.

Judging by statements made by various doctors and some of the other medical personnel at the hospital, it is clear that they have received specific instructions concerning Barinov. When questioned as to why he is not allowed to have visitors, they have all replied by citing instructions from 'higher up'. The doctors engaged in treating him explain their diagnosis of Barinov as insane by pointing out that he, a family man, is engaged in the lowest paid type of work; that he, a self-taught musician, founded a Christian rock musical group which, against all reason, is attempting to gain official permission to appear on stage in the USSR.

They added the cynical observation that if it proved impossible to build a sound criminal case against Barinov, he could always be declared insane.

Having received no reply from you to the open appeal we sent the Presidium earlier this year, we nonetheless are continuing our efforts to gain official permission for our group to appear in public, as is our right.

Millions of people both in our own country and abroad are both pleased and proud that a Christian music group such as the Trumpet Call has appeared in the Soviet Union. What are all these people likely to think when they learn that not only has the group gained no permission to perform, but that its founder has been forcibly placed into a psychiatric hospital?

This incarceration of Barinov as a means of putting a stop to his active, open profession of Christianity is a violation of the fundamental law of our land – the Constitution, which guarantees freedom of conscience and religious profession.

On behalf of the other members of the Trumpet Call group and Barinov's family and friends, I call upon you to give immediate sanction to the release of Valeri Barinov from psychiatric hospital, the sojourn in which may well have tragic consequences for him.

(signed) Sergei Timokhin   18th October, 1983

However, before Sergei's appeal had even reached Keston College, Valeri was released. Whenever I think about this, I am reminded of the story of Peter's miraculous escape from prison described in Acts. The key to Peter's release was prayer. What had the authorities hoped to achieve by incarcerating him in the first place? Did they simply intend to warn him, to terrify him into submission? Or did they simply want to prevent him physically from having any more contact with young people? Perhaps they thought that by declaring him insane they would discredit him and dissuade some of his followers from having further contact with him. Although he had been subjected to ten months of constant harassment, threats, detentions, interrogations, this was the first time they had applied physical torture. Obviously they wanted to see whether they could break his will.

As Sergei wrote in his appeal, Valeri had been given injections of aminazin from the first day of his admission into hospital. This drug is known in the West as largactil or thorazine. It is commonly used in the treatment of schizophrenia and related psychoses. A number of unpleasant side effects and complications can occur with its use, some of which may have irreversible results. These include a lowering of the blood pressure, jaundice, allergic skin reactions, abnormal skin pigmentation, weight gain, blurred vision and drowsiness.

These injections were stopped on 18th October after Tanya protested strongly to the doctor in charge of the section of the hospital in which Valeri was placed. She was told that Valeri's discharge or detention for 'further treatment' would be decided only after a medical commission could be convened to study his case. Valeri himself had been told upon admission that he would be there for at least a month while it was determined whether he was sane. When Tanya pressed the doctors to give the reason for Valeri's detention they replied: 'Your husband's views on religion differ so much from those of ordinary Soviet citizens that he is in need of psychiatric treatment'. Sergei referred in his appeal to the fact that the doctors regarded the possibility of declaring Valeri insane as an alternative to his being convicted as a criminal. The spell in hospital may simply have been intended as a means of keeping Valeri out of the way while a suitable criminal case was prepared against him. Whatever the motive, in this particular instance it did not work.

Valeri's release on 20th October came after only ten days in detention. Valeri and his friends attributed this firstly to the prayers that had been offered on his behalf and secondly to the considerable amount of publicity given to the case in the West. There must have been great rejoicing in the Barinov household on that day. How did

146

the news reach Keston College? In a telephone conversation with a staff member at the College a friend of the Barinovs reported that he had seen Barinov on the metro on the morning of 20th October with Zhanna and Marina. They were on their way home. 20th October happens to be Zhanna's birthday. What a marvellous present, even though a shadow was cast over the celebrations by the news that now Sergei was in trouble. On the same day he was informed officially that a criminal case was being prepared against him. Its basis appeared to be a complaint from unnamed 'neighbours' that he was engaging in the private production and sale of clothing. No charge was ever brought against him on this, but he had to live with the threat that this would happen.

What impact did Valeri's unexpected release have on the Leningrad Church? Several months after the event Valeri recorded a message on tape and sent it to Keston College. He said the following:

> When I was in psychiatric hospital, the whole Leningrad Church prayed for me. Although they didn't understand my way of evangelism, they still loved me as a brother. When the Lord rescued me from hospital, they greeted me with great joy. This was a spiritual victory for the church. Even though the elders were against me, everyone knew immediately that they had witnessed an act of God. Perhaps they will never understand my mission, but they understood one thing – that I am their brother in Christ and shall always be so.

One might have expected that Valeri, after the experience of the previous ten days, would have tried to keep a low profile for a while. But not Valeri. Within days he was making preparations for a big evangelistic meeting.

News of his release from hospital had spread around town and people were more curious than ever to come and hear what this rock star Christian had to say. On 11th November at eight-thirty in the evening some 200 young people gathered near the Leningrad Baptist Church. As in the past, this group included many of the city's drop-outs, drug addicts, heavy drinkers and prostitutes. Presumably Valeri had warned the church authorities about the meeting beforehand, but they were evidently not happy about it. The church Presbyter, Konovalchik, and Anatoli Morozov flatly refused them admittance. Valeri had to think quickly or he would lose this opportunity to witness to 200 people. They would not stand around in the freezing cold for very long.

By that time, Valeri had given up his job as a maintainer of skating rinks and become a night watchman on a building site. Suddenly the thought occurred to him to take the assembled group to the Working Men's Club on the building site. The word was quickly passed round the crowd and eventually about eighty people moved off with Valeri and Sergei and the rest of the crowd dispersed.

The meeting in the club soon got underway in an orderly fashion. There were testimonies and Bible readings. Everyday problems were discussed and Christian solutions offered. After an hour the meeting was abruptly ended. A fleet of black marias roared up to the club which was quickly surrounded by a militia unit, headed by a Major Ivanov, and a number of plain-clothes men from the KGB. All the people present were loaded into the militia vans and driven away for questioning. Among them was Zhanna Barinova who was then just fourteen. No exception was made for her, despite the fact that she was a minor. Most of the people were questioned and released without too much delay. The ringleaders, Valeri, Sergei and one of their friends, were held for over three hours and released after two a.m.

About a week later Valeri was summoned for an interview with a special commission of psychiatrics. Valeri described this interview in a tape-recorded message which he managed to send abroad several months later.

A month after my release from psychiatric hospital I was summoned to a special psychiatric commission. I was asked the following question: 'Valeri, you know that in our country there is religious liberty. Can you tell us why, among the vast majority of believers, you alone have attracted such attention to yourself?' I gave the following reply: 'I've been attending the Baptist Church in Leningrad since 1971. I've noticed that our best preachers are suppressed while the less talented ones preach. As a rule, their sermons are aimed at the elderly and are totally unacceptable to young people today. This church, set up under the pressure of compulsory atheism, suits our government very well because they hope that the old generation of believers will die out and young people will know nothing about God. In this way the church will cease to exist. Because I was aware of this terrible situation I had the idea of forming a Christian rock group and using modern music as a means of communicating the gospel to young people I praise God that now, just as our first religious work is beginning to circulate throughout the country, there's a great spiritual awakening among young people. This is the real reason why Sergei Timokhin and I are being persecuted by the authorities. They have forced many people, including you psychiatrists, to pay special attention to us. Not only to us, but to all active Christians who want good for their people.

In response to this bold statement Valeri was informed by the commission that they did not consider him 'fully well'. It is clear from the second part of the recorded message that harassment by the staff at the PND continued unabated. During the course of subsequent interviews with psychiatric staff, Valeri was questioned closely about his connections with foreigners and particularly with Keston College.

Sergei and I prayerfully await a time of blessing from the Lord when he will give an opportunity for our group, Trumpet Call, to work and to sing about the coming of Christ. In the meantime, our situation is difficult. The authorities are determined to deal with us harshly and are actively preparing falsified material. Even so, for the time being, the words of one of the KGB agents, who interviewed us at the beginning of the year have not come true. He said, in the presence of an official at the CRA, Nikolai Kirov, that we would be sent to the Ural mountains, turned into dissidents and that our wives and children would be the most wretched people. So far they have prevented Sergei from getting permanent work, so that they can label him a parasite and put him in prison. They put me on the list of psychiatric patients without examining me and later forcibly put me away in a mental hospital with the aid of the militia. The nurse, Yudina, constantly calls at my home and demands that I go immediately to see the head doctor, Kizeev, at the PND. At the same time she insults me, calling me a braggart and a traitor. If I'd been really ill they wouldn't have treated me in that way. The medical orderly who handed me over to the hospital in the presence of the district militiaman, Uvarov, and a few duty militiamen from the 36th section, laughed at me and tried to intimidate me by wishing me the most painful Golgotha.

Following the 'Christian evening' which we organised on 11th November, many people were persecuted. For example, a number of third-year students were expelled from the Leningrad Theological Seminary, among them Father Seraphim. At INR–91* where Sergei and I work as night watchmen and where we held our gathering because the authorities would not allow the young people to meet in the church, our boss received a telephone call from Major Andreichenkov. He ordered the dismissal of Alexei Orlov, one of the night watchmen, for his religious convictions. Because our people are afraid of the KGB the boss immediately dismissed him. They told him that they were laying him off because

___

* Presumably the number of the building site where Valeri was employed.

there was not enough work and they no longer needed him. However, after he had left three new watchmen were appointed in his place.

Not long after I was summoned to the school attended by my elder daughter, Zhanna. She had also been present at the 'Christian evening'. The teachers who had sent for me appeared to be good people. They said they had been informed by the militia that Zhanna had been found guilty of 'disturbing public order' on 11th November. I had to explain everything to them, starting at the beginning with the formation of Trumpet Call and all the consequences of my having composed a purely religious work. I told them about my spell in psychiatric hospital and the fact that the KGB had even followed the girls to school. When I had finished, everything was clear to them and they had only one comment to make: 'Have pity on your children'. That response, 'Have pity on your children' meant one thing: the sinister mechanism of atheism stops at nothing and is not afraid even to cripple children's souls. It's terrible to think that these evil forces are always going to be there, admittedly not in the foreground, but they put ordinary people in jeopardy and thereby warp their souls. I am sorry for these teachers at school 101, for the psychiatrists at the Skvortsov Stepanov hospital, the boss of the department at INR–91. I'm sorry for all those through whom the KGB works. They are most to be pitied, as indeed are all those who live without God. Christ is praying for them to his heavenly father even to this day: 'Father, forgive them for they know not what they do'.

Sergei and I wrote just two complaints to the Presidium of the Supreme Soviet, one about our illegal detention by the militia at the Moscow station in January and a second one about my compulsory internment in psychiatric hospital. In both cases, we received the same answer: no illegal action whatsoever had been taken by the authorities. We realised that there was no point in continuing to complain to the government as we would then simply be labelled anti-Soviet agitators and slanderers. But what kind of anti-Soviet agitators are we? If our socialist system were set up for our benefit, naturally we should work with pleasure for the good of our people, in co-operation with the communist party, because our aim is to do all we can to make our fellow human beings better people, cleansed from sin through Jesus Christ, and therefore more useful to society.

Finally, in the name of all the people who have been crushed by crude atheism we beg you to help us so that these evil forces cannot extinguish the fire of spiritual awakening which is flaring up in our land. The help we need most is prayer. May God bless you all. To him be eternal praise.

Thousands of Christian parents in the Soviet Union face the same dilemma that confronted Tanya and Valeri. What will the consequences of our actions as Christians be for our children? We have had no evidence that the Barinov girls have been victimised by teachers or disadvantaged in any way at school, but many Christian children in the Soviet Union do suffer because of their parents' beliefs.

Certainly, among their school friends, Zhanna and Marina must have achieved a certain notoriety, albeit not one they would have chosen. By December 1983 a rumour was going around town that Valeri was secretly involved in drug trafficking.

In an attempt to analyse the significance of this latest KGB tactic a staff member of Keston College, wrote the following:

Spreading the story that the Trumpet Call members are trafficking in drugs is an obvious attempt by the KGB to discredit the group. One can assume that the authorities hope to blacken Valeri Barinov's name even further with official Baptists (some of whom in the Leningrad congregation are sympathetic to Barinov and the others) and possibly scare off young people who are showing keen interest in spiritual things, particularly since the news of Barinov's forced internment in a psychiatric hospital in October and his subsequent unexpected, quick release reached them via foreign radio broadcasts to the USSR. Perhaps, too, the KGB hope that the old adage 'if enough mud is slung some will stick' will work to make people in the West wonder if Barinov and the group are legitimate.

Perhaps even more worrying is the speculation that this may be a prelude to bringing charges against Barinov for drug trafficking, which would carry a maximum sentence of ten years. It would not be unknown for the KGB to go so far as to plant drugs on a believer and then arrest him. This has happened at least four times in the past few years. In July 1981 Jewish believer Stanislav Zubko was sentenced to four years' camp after narcotics and a firearm were 'discovered' in his flat. Galina Vilchinskaya, 24-year-old daughter of a Baptist pastor, was arrested in November 1982 and charged with possession of drugs which had been 'found' in her luggage during an airport security check. A third incident involved another religious Jew, Lev Elbert. He was charged with possession of drugs supposedly found in his jacket when he arrived at the labour camp where he was to serve a one-year sentence. There is, therefore, precedent for such a set-up.

Valeri and the group were undaunted by the rumours. At the beginning of December they sent an appeal to the West announcing that they would conduct a week of prayer and fasting leading up to Christmas Day, during which they would ask God to grant them further opportunities for evangelism among alcoholics and drug addicts in the city. The appeal concluded with these words:

We ask you to remember us in your prayers as you

153

prepare to celebrate the birth of our Lord, who brought the light of salvation to all men and whose love extends to all, even the lowest and most wretched. We ask for the support of your prayers that we may continue to bring the joy of his message of salvation to those who stand in greatest need of it.

Some weeks after the terrifying experience of enforced psychiatric confinement followed by his release, Valeri's heart was overflowing with thanks to God and despite renewed pressure it is clear that he was determined to press on with his work. He obviously felt that one of the obstacles in his path was his relationship with the leaders at the church and some members of the congregation. This was a subject for urgent prayer. Valeri describes what happened as follows:–

On about 15th December the Lord prompted me to go and confess my sins in front of the whole church. I went out into the middle of the aisle at the front and I said, so everyone could hear: 'Lord, today you have prompted me to confess my sins before you and before the whole church'. I knew that the elders badly wanted me to confess, but what they wanted me to say was that I would give up my evangelistic work, that it was not 'of God' and that the group was not 'of God' and so on. So I phrased my confession as follows: 'Lord, if the prophets repented before you with dust and ashes what does this signify for me? Forgive me – I am a sinner'. Then I addressed the body of the church and said: 'I want the church to understand me. Perhaps some have been tempted because of me, perhaps some are harbouring ill feeling or are offended because of me. I beg you, brothers and sisters, to forgive me. I love you all sincerely.' I feel that this was a great victory. Afterwards everyone embraced me. But my aim is not to be reinstated in the church. I don't consider myself excluded from the church. In my prayer I also said the following: 'Thank you, Lord, that the church prayed for me, and you, Lord, delivered me from psychiatric hospital; Lord, I beg you, that the church will bless me in the future, because my only desire is to live for you, to live for your church and for my brothers and sisters'.

Valeri's confession was not necessarily what the elders wanted to hear, but it helped to break down some of the barriers that existed and to reconcile him with some members of the congregation who had been critical of him.

8: Rally to the Call

What was the evidence upon which Valeri Barinov based his bold assertion that people, and especially young people, were beginning to wake up from a spiritual slumber brought about by atheism? I shall answer this question by quoting directly from many of the seventy letters which were received by Valeri and Sergei in response to the BBC Russian Service broadcasts and which eventually found their way into the Keston College archive.

The letters fall roughly into three categories, though their ideas overlap:

1) letters from people who state that they are not believers;
2) letters from believers;
3) letters from people who do not mention personal religious convictions or the religious aspect of *The Trumpet Call* in their letters.

As we read these letters, we are prying into something very personal. We see into the souls of young people. Many of them may not be aware of it, but what they express is a spiritual yearning. Man's search for his true identity as a being created in the image of God takes on a new dimension in a society where the opposite of Christianity is taught, where the spiritual realm is denied and the material lauded to the skies. Soviet citizens are educated to think of themselves as builders of communism, part of a collective, and the idea of an individual spiritual pilgrimage is considered negative, or even subversive.

However, no political system can destroy the inner part of man, the spirit. It will not be distorted or manipulated irrevocably by lies or deceit. Nearly seven decades of communist indoctrination have been singularly unsuccessful in eradicating religious faith or a search for belief in God.

The following extracts will give something of the flavour of the correspondence. One young man exchanged a number of letters with Valeri, posing a whole series of questions about God and Christianity.

In the first letter he wrote:

You write that after the death of the body, the soul lives on. Can this really be true? I would like to be able to believe this.

Some time later, after he had received a cassette recording of *The Trumpet Call* and a letter from Valeri he wrote:

About God: previously I had not given this much thought. It was your letter, and what I heard about your group on the BBC, that made me think seriously for the first time in my life. You say that true happiness is to live for the glory of Christ, for others. Maybe I, too, will one day come to this understanding. . . . All these thoughts have been awakened, in the first instance, by your songs.

This letter from the first category is typical of many writers who profess that their interest in Christianity has been aroused either through hearing about *The Trumpet Call* on the BBC or through receiving a tape of a music and letters from Valeri and Sergei. It is clear from the comments and questions contained in the letters that the musicians went to great lengths to explain the fundamentals of their faith in God.

Of the twenty people who write declaring either that they are non-believers or that they believe in another religion or philosophy, every single one poses at least one question about the Christian faith. Some express their feelings and doubts with great perception and clarity, such as the writer of the following letter, a fifteen-year-old schoolboy living about 150 miles north of Moscow.

My attitude towards religion and god* is very positive, as I think that this brings people happiness. I would put myself in the category of 'wavering believers'. In other words, those who believe in god, and yet don't believe. I'll try to explain. Let's say I believe in god, but at the same time I do not do this actively. I'm not fighting to promote the idea. And indeed, this faith is somehow a spontaneous one, a sort of subconscious feeling. One might say: if the soul feels the presence of god, that means he exists. But this, too, is somehow induced, or is even a self-delusion. For example, let's say a person hears and finds out about god for the first time. If nobody leads him astray, he will carry this faith (for upon encountering god for the first time he will surely believe) through his entire life. And not a single doubt will ever appear in his heart about the existence of god. But the world is not without evil people. And atheist citizens start spouting all sorts of things: that there is no such thing as the supernatural, that all religion is rubbish, and so forth. And the first doubt begins to stir in people's souls, and they start to wonder: maybe what I believe in really is a delusion? And this can become a kind of fixed idea which can be nursed along until the believer becomes an atheist. Even the most sincere believers must have this doubt somewhere deep inside them, in the very bottom of their soul. By sincere believers I mean those who go to church, pray, observe the fasts, and so on. As for the doubts I have

* Written with a small letter in the original (as always in the Soviet press).

158

mentioned, I think that many of them flourish because people lack information, are ignorant about religion, are unable to understand its finer points. Many have never so much as seen a Bible (myself for one), and isn't the Bible the main source of all religious information?

. . . By the way, could you explain to me what the difference is between catholics and baptists or protestants? Everywhere around us we see the struggle of ideas and convictions, between religion and atheism also. One lot says there is god, the other maintains that there isn't. Both sides present evidence to back up their point of view, believe whom you will. As for me, I always try to get to the basic truth of every matter in order to know for sure: this is the truth and this is a lie.

Although I'm far from god, I'm quite clear in my mind that religion brings only good, and nothing bad to people. It brings out the best in them, raises them, encourages them to forsake bad ways, makes the good even better: all this comes from belief in god. Moreover not from fear of punishment, but from an inner need to do good and help other people. It's a great pity that our government doesn't understand, and doesn't want to understand, such a simple thing. If the Trumpet Call were to be allowed to perform publicly, to become known, people would start to think about the message in your songs, seek the path of truth and become *real human beings*. Still our authorities are blind in this matter, as in everything else. In any case, our government is absolutely useless. If they can't see when something is to their benefit, what can one expect? No wonder the whole country is in such a mess. . . .

No one would agree more wholeheartedly than Valeri with this boy's perceptive comment about doubts flourishing as a result of ignorance, lack of information and the non-availability of the Bible. It is a theme which recurs frequently in Valeri's own writing. Like this boy who 'always tried to get to the basic truth of every matter in order to know for sure what is the truth and what is a lie', many of the writers describe their personal struggle to 'seek the truth'.

I'm 27 years old and I work as a machine-setter in a factory. Before that, until 1976, I did this in a factory producing sewing machines. The work I do now is a bit more complicated and the money (from which there is no getting away!) is enough for my needs. I'm not married and do not expect to be in the foreseeable future, but who knows? I've been a member of the Komsomol since 1976, that is, from the time I started my present job. I didn't want to join, but considerable pressure was exerted to make me do so. It's not that I mind paying Komsomol dues – it's just that my convictions don't tally with theirs. I don't consider myself politically knowledgeable, but I do know the difference between good and evil. I seem to be using the word 'but' an awful lot, and that isn't very good.

My spiritual life can be described as one error and sin after another, though that may depend on how one looks at it. As I understand it, you neither smoke nor drink. I smoke, although I managed to stop drinking with medical assistance. Maybe that was facilitated by my own inner feelings. What the future holds, I don't know. You're right when you say that excessive drinking is both unhealthy and wrong. I know that from personal experience, moreover, I know how much grief I brought my mother because of this.

My closest friend (. . .), a medical student in Kalinin, is crazy about Led Zeppelin and the Beatles, who are my favourite group as well. I like John Lennon best of all of them, even though he once declared himself an atheist. Still, that's beside the point. He wanted peace and happiness for all, and that's what is most important.

Maybe that's why he's no longer among the living. In my heart, however, he'll always be alive. As I write, I can't help trying to recall which rock musicians were believers, or professed to be (to put it crudely). The first who comes to mind is Cliff Richard, a Christian. Bob Dylan became a Christian despite the fact that he is, I believe, a Jew, and therefore could have been expected to follow Judaism. George Harrison was much attracted to Hinduism and I've heard that David Bowie was all set to become a Buddhist monk, but conquered this urge and remained a rock musician. But these are just my recollections.

It's probably clear to you by now that I'm not, myself, a believer: nonetheless, I share many of your views. I, personally, derived no spiritual gain from the Komsomol, and I'm not afraid to write these words. There's still much falsehood, injustice and vice in our world. Many are fighting this only to fall into the same errors.

There was a girl whom I fancied for a long time, but now there seems to be a chasm between us: this summer she finishes a correspondence course at a technical institute, she joined the Party a year ago and is now a minor official – in other words, she's begun her ascent on the professional ladder, and I'm just a plain mortal. Admittedly, a lot of our views clashed and now, thank god, we seem set to go our separate ways with our separate ideas. So you see – no luck in love for me.

Still, I hope the future holds better things. I hope that I'll be able to become a better person, morally cleaner, I suppose you could call it. I hope that I shall not do harm to others either by word or deed. Maybe your rock opera, if I manage to hear it, will help me.

Other writers revealed almost nothing about their personal lives, but came straight to the point:

By chance I heard a musical programme presented by Seva Novgorodtsev on 23rd April 1983. At the end he read out your address and I decided to write to you. We learned of the difficulties and obstacles your group is facing. Unfortunately, we were unable to hear your song which was played because the broadcast was jammed too thoroughly. From what could be made out it seems that your group is a Christian one. How do you explain this, and what does religion give you? We should so much like to hear more of the music you've written. I would very much like to correspond with you regularly. If possible, please reply to this letter at the following address. . . .

The above letter, dated 23rd April 1983, was followed just over a month later by a second one from the same writer:

I received your letter and will send you a cassette as soon as you can let me know Sergei Timokhin's patronymic: the post office here refuses to accept packages without the full name of the addressee. I would very much like to know how your songs reached England, and how you manage to have contact with Seva Novgorodtsev. In what style do you perform your songs? You write that there is plenty of evidence for the presence of god in the universe, but what is this evidence? Until next time! I await your reply!

Other comments contained in several of the letters express unanimous sympathy with the aims of Christianity. The following extracts are all taken from letters in the first category, addressed to Sergei:

Thank you very much for your letter. Regards to your friends and family. What a wonderful thing it is that the Trumpet Call exists. I thought it was just something Seva had made up. Like you, I'm 25 years old and married. As yet we have no children. I'm not a believer

myself, but I'm not against believers in any way. . . .
The voice of your group will help many to find the true
path in life. On this, I'll close. I wish you all success.
As for god – maybe he does exist after all. . . .

I'm a total stranger to you, writing from the distant city
of Kirov. My name is.... While listening to the BBC, I
heard about your group for the first time. I've been a
regular listener to this programme for a long time, not
just for the musical content, but with the aim of
studying how broadcasts of this type are presented in
the West. . . . I was stunned to hear about your group,
your aims and your hopes. You're the first musicians
I've encountered who are fired by a single ideal to the
core of your being. I know that you've now gained great
popularity and probably receive a lot of mail. . . . You
know, I don't believe in god, but your songs interest
me greatly.

Having received a reply from Sergei, the above author
wrote again with various observations about Christianity
and further questions:

Thank you very much for your letter. In all truth, I
didn't expect a reply. Thank you again! I'm sending a
cassette at the same time as I post this letter.

I read your letter with care in order to understand
correctly the concepts you set out in it. It seems to me
that I've understood what it is that you see as your faith
in God. It's not for me to tell you the history of religion,
but it seems to me that your faith in Christ is that
same faith which appeared among people wishing for
something bright and happy in their future life. A faith
in something exalted, unsoiled by clerics. This is not
just my opinion. I've discussed your letter at length
with my friends and played that piece of your music
which I had managed to record during its airing on the
BBC. I must tell you that you have our wholehearted

support. . . . I read your letter over and over, thinking about your arguments in favour of God.

The way in which Valeri and Sergei have been able to enter into such an open and honest correspondence with so many of these young people clearly indicates the need for a pastoral ministry among 'wavering believers' and how admirably they could fulfil this role if they were permitted to do so. This need is clearly not being met adequately within the existing churches (and of course in many places there are none). Given the severe restrictions which operate and the enormous difficulty even of forming a Christian discussion group, these strictures are hardly surprising. The penalties for the organisers of unofficial activities are severe. The tragic demise of the Christian Seminar which began in Moscow in 1977 is a case in point. More recently there was the cruel treatment of Alexander Riga, a Roman Catholic who was incarcerated in a psychiatric hospital in 1984 for holding Bible study classes for young people.

The letters I have quoted provide clear evidence that Valeri's talk of 'spiritual awakening' was not idle fantasy. His desire was to reach precisely this category of young people, who, for whatever reason, were not particularly attracted to going to church. He knew from personal experience from his years in Western Siberia how difficult it is to grow spiritually without a caring fellowship where you can be taught the basics of the Christian faith and learn to share it with others.

It is obvious that Valeri's music stimulated many people who at some time in their lives had thought about religious faith seriously, to examine the claims of Christianity. It would have been impossible for Valeri and Sergei to answer all these questions adequately, even if they had sufficient knowledge to do so. Valeri would be the first to admit that his theological knowledge would never earn him a degree. But they have learned from life. Both men tried to share their own living experience of God, the reality of Christ's power for them personally. They tried to go beyond the realm of theory and challenged their readers to prove for themselves the existence of God. They did not ask them to do anything they had not done themselves. Their view is that God can and does reveal himself through the Holy Spirit to people in many different ways. But they were very conscious of the weight of responsibility in responding sensitively and adequately to such a wide range of questions and statements.

Some of their replies drew immediate responses, but the letter writing must have been extremely time-consuming and to some extent frustrating, because they often found themselves replying to the same type of question over and over again. This prompted Valeri firstly to write an 'open letter' to Seva's audience which Seva broadcast on 30th April 1983. Secondly, he recorded a series of sermons on tape which he sent to the West in which he tried to deal with the themes which had occurred most frequently in the letters. Some extracts from these sermons were broadcast over foreign radio stations.

Without exception all the letter-writers express their admiration for Valeri's music, for his achievement, and they ask for a full recording of *The Trumpet Call*. Out of the total of seventy letters there are only two mild criticisms of *The Trumpet Call* as a musical work. Many of them express their views about the Soviet rock scene and list their favourite Western bands. From some of the comments one can deduce that not all Soviet young people are happy with the homegrown variety of rock music and this explains partly why they listen so avidly to Western broadcasts of pop music. Many of the writers comment scathingly on Soviet pop groups. This is not the only aspect of Soviet society about which they are unhappy – many of them drop veiled or even open hints about other unsatisfactory features of the Soviet way of life, including the postal system.

If these letters had been written by a group of Western young people, one could be forgiven for thinking they were slightly crazy, obsessed about an imaginary 'enemy within' who is bent on monitoring all their contacts, but in the Soviet Union censorship is a fact of life. It is not surprising that so many writers express doubts about whether their letters will actually arrive and whether they will arrive intact. There is some censorship on domestic mail, as well as strict censorship on letters arriving from and being sent abroad. There is an element of risk attached to writing to somebody who is clearly officially disapproved of by the authorities. As is often the case in societies where all kinds of censorship operate and people cannot express themselves freely, often the best way forward is humour or satire.

I have designated the letters in the third category as coming from people who do not make any reference to Christianity or religion. This does not mean, of course, that none of them believes or is sympathetic to Christianity – there is simply no indication of their attitudes in this regard. These letters – there are only nine of them – none the less contain some revealing and sometimes amusing comments on rock music and Soviet society. It is also interesting that, regardless of their views on religion, so many of them clearly want to express solidarity, even to the extent of sending money.

I don't know whether you listened to the BBC musical programme presented by Vsevolod Novgorodtsev last Saturday, of which ten minutes were devoted to your group. I heard this programme as a regular listener. . . . The fact that your open letter reached the West is already an enormous achievement for your group: the fact that it was included in the programming of the Russian service of the BBC is a double achievement, because that means you will acquire an enormous following in the USSR and I'm sure that my letter is just one of many you'll receive. (I can only hope that this letter reaches you without any untoward 'adventures'.) I hope that all the other letters will reach you, and it's my guess that you, too, proceeded in a manner not calculated to add an extra burden to the already lousy operation of Soviet official post.

. . . That's all. I look forward to your answer soon.* Write to me at the following box number. . . . And again, this time in Russian: I look forward to your reply. One other thing – be sure to send your letter by registered post or with advice of delivery, otherwise it's unlikely to reach me. 14th March 83. Tula.

* * * *

We were listening recently to Seva and heard a piece by your Trumpet Call group, which we liked very much as we are fans of 'hard rock'. In our opinion, yours is the first Soviet group to meet all the requirements of this branch of music. We liked the originality of the actual performance and the quality of the voices. . . We are both 19 years old.

With all best wishes,

* * * *

Personally, I think you are not acting wisely: much better keep a low profile, record your songs on the quiet and let them spread among the masses. Still, I hope you've had no more unpleasantness.

* * * *

Greetings to all the members of the Trumpet Call. I greet you on this day of international solidarity of workers. What can I wish for you? I hope that the sound of your trumpets won't be silenced, that international society won't abandon you in your time of need, and that the workers of other countries will really demonstrate their solidarity with you. Happy May Day, boys! On the matter of financial assistance† . . . well, as Seva Novgorodtsev said, 'the sending of money by post is a delicate business, a political one. One careless move

---

* These two sentences are written in English.
† A reference to the fact that his 'Open letter' read over the air on 30th April, stated that he and Sergei were in financial difficulties.

and they will fabricate a case against you for three kopecks'. . . .

★　★　★　★

I'm a music-lover and therefore frequently listen to the radio (I'm sure you know what I mean!). I'd already heard about your group (on the radio, of course) and then – what a coincidence! On 30th April Seva read out your open letter and the very next day someone brought me a cassette with your concert on it. That was just too much for the heart of an old rocker like me! So I decided to write to you. At last we have our own really good indigenous hard-rock group! One can only regret that it must turn immediately for help to 'the workers, the students and the fearless'. You should have kept more of a low profile. Still, it's no use crying over spilt milk, and all you can do now is carry on as you have begun. The young people of Rostov are with you in spirit.

Unfortunately money can't be sent in the mail, so expect a postal transfer from me soon to the sum of ten roubles – it's all I can afford at the moment. . . .

★　★　★　★

Returning to the letters in the first category, many of these writers, apart from asking questions and expressing their views on religion, also have plenty to say about the other issues we have mentioned above. It is obvious from the letters already quoted that a major talking point of these young people is how to obtain a supply of good blank cassette tapes. They also contain some pleasing touches of black humour:

I'm a lover of rock music. On the BBC pop programme of 12th March 1983 I heard about your Trumpet Call group, your open letter and the consequences of it. I was most interested in your song which was played on this programme. Unfortunately, it's unlikely that you'll be permitted to perform in public before the Second Coming of Christ, and certainly nothing like this is envisaged in the current five-year plan! And I'd so much like to hear your work in full.

If possible, please send me a cassette with the songs performed by the Trumpet Call. Naturally, I'll cover all the expenses.

Please write in any case. . . .

The writer of the above letter received a reply from Valeri and then wrote back immediately.

I received your letter on 30th March – thank you for writing. Quite honestly, I didn't really expect to get a reply. . . . Soviet rock music is improving, but it still has a long way to go before it reaches world class: maybe the Trumpet Call will prove to be an exception?

It's a very good thing that you and your friends have found your ideal in Christ, but it seems to me that everyone believes in the supernatural when going through difficult times, though not necessarily in God as a source of aid.

One day I read an article about Seva Novgorodtsev in the *Rovesnik** magazine and, naturally, started listening to his programmes. That article must have gained him a lot of new listeners, contrary to its intention!

I sent you a blank cassette on 31st March and look forward to getting it back with your music on it.

Well, that's it. I wish you every success.

A good number of blank cassette tapes were obviously

* *The Contemporary*, a journal for young people which published a slanderous article about Seva Novgorodtsev.

being forwarded to Leningrad and someone must have been kept very busy copying tapes. But for many of the young people just getting hold of a blank cassette was a major problem. This is mentioned by more than a third of the writers:

> It's virtually impossible to get tapes here at the moment. If you could do a tape for me yourself, I'll pay you for it, or send you a clean one in exchange once the 'tape crisis' resolves. Save tape by just sending me the Russian version of your work.

For this young man at least, the 'tape crisis' was eventually solved, as his subsequent letter indicates:

> You know, I recently visited Kashin (a town about 630 km from Kalyazin where I live), went into the 'Household Goods' shop and what did I see? 'Maxwelle'* cassettes (though possibly the labels are only copies) each capable of recording 90 minutes, selling for only 10 roubles 50 kopecks (£10)! The salesman told me they had been lying around for about a month. If you or anyone else would like some, send money as quickly as possible before they're all sold (I doubt that I am richer than you). Must stop now. Belated Easter greetings to you, regards to the others. I know how difficult things must be right now for you, but remain firm. As they say in one of Grand Funke's songs, 'Good times will come'. You know that you can always rely on us.

> God keep you.

* * * *

I was most impressed by your performance, even though audibility of the broadcast left much to be

---

* Presumably Maxell, which are considered, in the USSR, to be the best possible.

desired. It would be a great treat to obtain a tape of
your music. I've a big favour to ask of you: please tape
it for me on the two cassettes I've sent you. It's terribly
hard to get magnetic tapes here. Therefore, I've had to
send used tapes. If you wouldn't be offended, I'd be
willing to pay for your time and efforts. Your group
would be known in Moscow and Leningrad, but here
in the eastern areas it is unlikely that many would know
about it. So I feel that to spread your work through all
available channels could play an important part in the
future of the group. I think you are hardly likely to
receive permission to perform publicly from the authorities. We hear a lot of loud talk about the rights of the
individual, but I don't think there's much of this in
practice.

★   ★   ★   ★

Greetings from Tula! My friend and I were listening
recently to the music programme broadcast from
London by Seva Novgorodtsev and heard about your
group. Your open letter was read out, and we were
most disturbed by it. We heard about your life, how
you've been kept under surveillance and forbidden to
perform in public. It was also stated that you were all
believers and sing about god in your songs. One of your
songs was played, but not right through to the end.
Therefore we decided to write to you.

So here we are. Unfortunately, we were unable to get
hold of a 1½ hour cassette as specified, so we have
bought two smaller ones. We would very much like to
have your songs in Russian on one cassette and in
English on the other. We hope you can do this. We
enclose a small sum of money, as we know you're having
financial problems. We're all human and should help
each other in difficult times. We shall try to send you
some more money later. We look forward to hearing
from you soon.

★   ★   ★   ★

Despite the genuine expression of solidarity and support, many of the young people were obviously dismayed that Valeri and Sergei had opted for such a high profile and thereby exposed themselves to harassment from the Soviet authorities. Several expressed their anger about the persecution that Valeri and Sergei had had to endure and others were pessimistic about what the future would hold for the Trumpet Call.

I heard about your group on Seva Novgorodtsev's show and liked your music very much, even though the quality of the recording itself is not very good. Still, that's understandable, as you had to work in such difficult circumstances.

I'm not a religious believer myself, but consider the persecution of people for their religious (or political) convictions absolutely disgusting. After all, the principles of Christianity must be close to the heart of any decent person. The refusal of the authorities to allow you to perform in public is not just a breach of the law, it's a breach of elementary moral norms. It's a shameful thing that you were forced to undergo a psychiatric examination, but the shame is not yours, it's the authorities who are shamed by this act.

There are not many people in our country who are willing to fight openly for their rights. I'm filled with admiration for you and wish you all the very best. Don't lose heart. . . .

I became extremely interested in your Trumpet Call group and in you, its members. Judging by everything I heard, you're very good people; you wish to undertake a very praiseworthy and engrossing activity. Still, as you've seen for yourself, in our country, unlike the West, everything is bogged down with petty formalities: we'll all have to ask special permission soon if we want so much as to hammer a nail into the wall! Yes, you lot, you've really started something; now you'll either get the permission you're after or you'll find yourselves on the receiving end of many very unpleasant things. You've already experienced one consequence – the incident at the station. Now, as they say, you've only two options: either stand your ground no matter what, or turn tail and run before it is too late. It's my sincere wish that you will follow the first option. . . .

Greetings, if you really exist and are not just a figment of Seva Novgorodtsev's imagination! He read out your open letter in his last programme. If the BBC isn't lying, I think you've taken a silly course of action. Now there's no chance that you'll be given permission to perform. You'll be branded as 'agents of international imperialism' and so on. Although you state in your open letter that you don't sing about politics, you've committed a political act by your very appeal to world public opinion. You've openly shown your contempt for those Soviet bodies to which your letter is addressed.

I've a favour to ask of you: could you possibly send me a copy of your *Trumpet Call* if you can spare the four roubles? If you can't do this, or don't want to, for some reason, at least please write so I might know that your group really exists. I'd also very much like to have a photo of the group, even if you're not famous yet!

Sergei wrote to this young man and told him about the 'Open letter' which Seva read out on the BBC and also about the group's hopes of having *The Trumpet Call* released as a record abroad. He received this immediate but rather negative reply:

. . . But to get back to your group. You gave an interview to the BBC, wrote an open letter and will be publishing a record abroad. Before this, I think the authorities probably only kept a wary eye on you. Now you can say farewell to any future activity: they'll grind you into the ground. . . .

The author of the next letter, while being realistic about the difficulties involved, offered encouragement for Valeri and Sergei to press on with their objectives:

Recently I heard your group, the Trumpet Call. I think you're very good. I think you deserve to have access to a wider audience, but there are obstacles in the way. I'm something of a specialist on rock music, especially heavy rock. I personally have absolutely no chance of 'rising to the top' and, although I keep trying to find my way out of the blind alley in which I find myself, all I encounter is new barriers.

I know that you're believers and would like to assure you that I have a great respect for faith in god, although I'm not a believer myself, and you have my whole-hearted support. As for the fact that you combine your faith with rock music – this is a marvellous thing, both for the world of music and for religion.

The following letter from a 22-year-old, offers further encouragement:

I learned of the existence of the Trumpet Call with the aid of a contemporary means of mass communication, in other words, from the pop programme broadcast from London by our fellow-countryman Vsevolod Novgorodtsev. I'm full of admiration for your courage, your ideals and simply for you yourselves. I'm in total support of your aim to stage concerts and am ready to give you any assistance in my power, small as that may be. I'd be delighted to hear your repertoire and help in its distribution. I extend to you the hand of a friend and comrade-in-arms.

The following writer offers praise for the Trumpet Call

174

and withering comments about some Soviet rock groups.

We (all my friends and I) are delighted by the appearance of a new rock group in Russia. All of us are sick and tired of the rubbishy songs played on our radio and television day and night. It's enough for some 'singer' to perform one of these 'songs' and, even if he has a voice like a goat, the next thing you know is that he's making records and becomes officially 'popular'. Still, I daresay you know this just as well as I do, and even better how difficult it is for new musicians to remain true to their chosen way. Even the Time Machine group, once they appeared on TV, dropped anything controversial. Nowadays it's not prison which awaits rebels, but the rebels are short of brains. Anyway, enough of that. . . .

The final letter from which I shall quote before moving on to discuss the letters received from believers is, like so many of the others, full of encouragement, advice and good will:

I heard the programme in which Seva read out your letter and I think I know what's posing problems for your creativity (and I don't mean just the difficulties which are being placed in your way). I think there are other factors.

After all, your group is new, you haven't had time to make a name for yourselves, not everyone knows your music. It's essential that as many people as possible get to hear your work. One airing on the radio is hardly sufficient; moreover, Seva is limited in the amount of time he can devote to you in a 30-minute programme. I would advise you to play your work to as many friends, acquaintances and the general public as possible. That way the word will start to get around, interest will grow, opinions will be expressed. People will start to think about what they've heard. They'll start to comprehend the meaning and in the end will make the right decision, the right choice – where and with whom to go forth in life. To be honest with you, I don't think of myself as a religious person. I neither reject nor accept religion. From time to time I think about this, but at the moment I see it all rather vaguely.

. . . I was deeply disgusted by the behaviour of those persons mentioned in your letter*. I've had occasion to meet up with these people, too, and know what these KGB and Leningrad Psychiatric Hospital types are like. In my opinion, one lot have no business to be in uniform and the others to be in medical coats with red crosses. A uniformed official should symbolise a call for a social order, so that there will be fewer drunks on the streets, fewer black marketeers and other parasites, and doctors in white coats should direct their energies to the treatment of the genuinely ill. As for proclaiming a perfectly sane person mad just because he happens to believe in god – it's CRIMINAL.

. . . I urge all of you to carry on with your performances, recordings and so on. Your music is good, you obviously have talent and the content, I believe, will bring only good results.

Over one third of all the letters are from committed Christians and, as one would expect, they convey solidarity, love and support. Just as many in the 'wavering believers' category wanted to express their inner thoughts, doubts and aspirations in their letters, so too do the Christians. Many wanted simply to write about the miracle of salvation through Christ and affirm their own belief in God:

I heard about you by chance on the BBC broadcast. I

* Those who registered Barinov as a psychiatric patient.

was amazed that you disregard all external difficulties and witness to the truth of life and the search for God. This is so important for young people today: they must find him. No barriers or difficulties will be able to withstand the desire for a new life. I've found this path that leads to salvation. The path which Jesus Christ showed us. Only through him were my eyes opened to the truth in life.

. . . As for music – I like it very much, especially if it is the kind which awakens in Man the desire to seek the truth. I see rock as this sort of music, for it can penetrate right into your soul, take you away from the mundane, petty worries of everyday existence and stimulate you on to a high plane.

Others who had found some of the answers to their questions about life in the Christian faith were prompted by what they heard about the Trumpet Call to explain their own views and try to start a Christian dialogue. This type of exchange of view by letter assumes great significance in a society where Christian discussion groups are illegal. The following two letters are from young people who have a basic understanding of the Christian faith, but obviously want to broaden their knowledge and understanding:

I heard your open letters broadcast by the BBC and one of your songs, therefore I would like to ask you some questions. Firstly, do you believe in God, or do you just preach the idea of 'the son of god'? How do you feel about the church? I am a keen collector of old books and am therefore 'acquainted' with the Christian faith, both through the Bible in the original and such interpretations of it as *The Writings of the Blessed Tikhon*. I have devoted much thought to this matter, tried to 'set aside' that which seemed to me absurd and finally came to agree with the 'Christian teaching' promulgated by L.N. Tolstoy. It was he who said: 'God manifests himself in every rational person by the desire to do good to all creation – in individual beings, each of whom strives for his own well-being. . . . Consideration shows man that the optimum good for people, towards which all people strive, can be attained only in the maximum unity and harmony between them. And therefore, although the final aim of the life of the world is hidden from man, he nevertheless knows in what lies the most immediate task of the life of the world in which he is called to participate: this task is to replace divisions and disagreements in the world by unity and harmony' (Tolstoy, *Christian Teaching*, Part 1, Chapter 9).

I'd very much like to have a regular correspondence with you, if you're agreeable – I really would be most interested.

*   *   *   *

By pure chance I learned of the existence in Piter* of a Christian rock group, the Trumpet Call. These are truly joyous tidings not just for me, but for all those who've set out to search for true spiritual values.

'Never have the hearts of men felt so keenly the need to believe, nor understood so well with their minds the impossibility of believing,' said D.S. Merezhkovsky back at the end of the 19th century. These words are even more true in our time. Therefore, in my opinion, the greatest achievement of the Trumpet Call, and your individual achievement, is that you're helping thinking young people to overcome this dissonance. I know from personal experience just how vital this is.

I'm a 19-year-old student of foreign languages. Religious questions have interested me for a long time.

---

* Popular abbreviation of pre-revolutionary name of Leningrad (St Petersburg).

178

. . . I'm not really qualified to pass musical judgments, but I suspect that you're using music as a means to an end. And your aim is quite clear, an honourable aim indeed!

I'd be very interested to learn something about the history of your group, about your activities. But, most importantly, I'd like to know about the religious views of its members – your group. Please write – I'm not asking just out of idle curiousity. My address is. . . .

I sincerely hope that all the unpleasantness you've had from the authorities is behind you for good. May these words of Christ be always with you: 'Blessed are ye when ye shall be slandered and persecuted for my sake: rejoice and be glad, for great is your reward in Heaven. . . . So were the prophets persecuted who came before ye' (Matt. 5.11–12).

Several writers gave an indication of the impact of the Trumpet Call in their particular circle. The following two letters are from the same author; the first was written after hearing about the group and the second after hearing the recording.

In one of V. Novgorodtsev's pop programmes I heard your open letter to our authorities. I was quite stirred by it, especially as you raise the question of religion and music. . . . Many well-known rock musicians trace their musical education back to their churches, which develop moral consciousness, awake in people the desire for truth, peace and love. Your Christian music group, the Trumpet Call, has set itself an exceptionally honour-able aim, the aim of all humanity. This is a law of life, and only in its observance shall we be able to bring up a new and worthy generation. Naturally, this is not acceptable to some, and there will be those who will seek to place obstacles in your path, but can one further confuse a people which is already totally confused with

politics? Yet there is no trace of politics in your work
– it's Christianity, pure and simple. Yes, your aim is
truly honourable. Maybe you'll think it strange to get
such a letter from a total stranger. Don't be surprised,
for it's one more piece of evidence that you're not alone
in what you're trying to do, that people want to hear
music such as yours, that they have a need for it.

It's a pity there's no chance of hearing your songs.

Well, that's it. Once more, I wish you all the best and
hope that your wish to perform will come about. My
deepest gratitude to you.

★ ★ ★ ★

I've received your cassette and am delighted with it –
the songs are very interesting and have real meaning,
but, most importantly, contain what you won't always
hear about among young people – about God. Maybe,
when they hear your songs, many of them will realise
what it is that they've been missing and what they need
so much, for sincerity and truth come through God. I
wish your group every success in your very difficult
task, I hope your aims will be realised and that truth
will triumph. May the world be enlightened, and may
people live as Jesus Christ wished them to. I must
tell you that your *Trumpet Call* has already achieved a
considerable degree of popularity in our town and tapes
of your work are being passed from hand to hand.
Admittedly, some people find a certain likeness to some
Western groups in your work, but if melody is born in
the heart, it comes from God, so there's nothing
surprising if there are some such likenesses. It would
be much appreciated if you could write something about
your Christian musical group, the Trumpet Call.

Other writers revealed that Valeri and the members of the
Trumpet Call are by no means the only Christians aspiring
to preach the gospel through the medium of modern

music. We read about the existence of several bands and attitudes to them within the churches.

I greet you in the name of our Lord Jesus Christ! I . . . send you sincere Christian greetings. Thank God that he joined us all into one whole by the blood of his Son, and that we're all brothers and sisters, all one family in Christ. I'm writing to you mainly because I have a great desire to learn more about your group. I must tell you, I'm a bit of a musician myself. In our church we have a small instrumental group. We've only recently started playing, but we already have a lot of problems which at times appear insuperable. Our small group of young people found your appeal very inspiring. Contemporary Christianity really does need to be shaken up, to be roused out of its lethargy. Christians have begun to forget Christ's injunction to go out and preach the gospel to all nations. They're engrossed with themselves and have little time for thinking about souls in need of salvation. It's up to us young people to stand up and bring the light into the hearts of people, to lead them to Christ.

The following letter was signed by three men, all in their early twenties, who designate themselves as poet and manager of a Christian group, poet and singer-composer and chairman of a religious youth group, respectively:

Greetings, dear friends!

We listened to your compositions with great pleasure and were, quite naturally, delighted. There hasn't been a single musical group to reflect the interests of Orthodox youth.

Dear friends – this lack has finally been filled by the appearance of the Trumpet Call – we're proud of you!

For the further publicising of your work, please send

us tapes of your religious songs. Don't worry about expenses – everything will be fully reimbursed when you come to the 'big city' – Moscow.

May there be eternal peace among the peoples of the Earth.

Some writers give more detailed accounts about how they are able to use their musical talents in the context of Christian worship and are anxious to receive guidance from Valeri and Sergei about the role of popular music in church:

I greet you in the love of Our Lord Jesus Christ! Thank you for your letter, to which I am replying with a slight delay. You expressed some very good thoughts concerning the work of a Christian in your letter. It's true that all too frequently our human nature moves us to do what goes against the will of God, and it's because of this that our efforts prove fruitless. Yet when each is in his rightful place, we're capable of not only achieving much, but can make an even greater contribution to God's harvest. 'We are all the body of Christ, but individually, we are only members.' I'm a comparative newcomer to this path and I ask only that God direct me where he will. It's good to be able to devote one's youth to the service of Christ and how great shall be the reward if Christ, at his coming, should find us employed in his work! May he help us in this!

I shall write a little more about myself. I'm 18 years old, and in a year's time will complete my studies in a mechanical construction technical college. Although I was born into a religious family, I didn't come to accept Christ as my Saviour until the age of sixteen. I thank God that, through my parents, he showed me the road to Golgotha. As I wrote to you earlier, I play the bass guitar in a small musical group – there are four of us. We generally play at social functions and youth evenings. We play at prayer meetings only once or twice a year, as many in the congregation are a bit hostile to modern music. Still, we don't let that upset us, the main thing is to praise Christ from the depths of our hearts. I'd like to know what you think about the playing of popular music in church. What should be its place? What aims should it have? What is the best number of musicians for such performances? Please write what your views are on this: we're only starting, and need all the advice we can get. . . .

Others write to Valeri about how the Trumpet Call has challenged them to think about evangelism and how they intend to use it as a means of sharing their faith:

One of our brothers . . . gave me a cassette with your music on it. We're currently in the process of making further copies of it, but unfortunately our equipment isn't very good: just a couple of ordinary Sonata and Vesna tape recorders, but still, it's better than nothing. Some of the local believers have given your music a hostile reception, but innovations of any kind usually produce some kind of opposition. I consider our main task is to bring light to the world! If we call ourselves children of God, then we must do his holy will. There are some who consider that young people prefer classical music and will not 'take' to yours. Never mind, time will tell. I pray to God that he will send awakening to the young people in our area. I'm in the process of writing up a leaflet to accompany the tapes of your music which will help the listener to understand it and to gain some knowledge of Christ. As I understand it, the tape can be divided into the following 'sections':
1. The trumpet call is heard all over the world.
2. The world is steeped in sin and rejects God.
3. Man seeks a way out – 'What shall I do?'
4. 'Look at Golgotha', look at Christ.
I particularly like the part where a prayer can be heard through the music. May God help you along your

difficult path! I'll be praying for you and for an awakening in the entire Soviet Union.

It's my firm belief that this will come to pass. Best wishes to you from the young people here. 'Stand in the freedom given to you by Christ. . . .'

★　★　★

Timofei, Yura and I play electric guitars. Last week we decided to 'recall our childhood' and play something on mandolins. It turned out splendidly, but there are few, so few, who play as you do. I've heard that the theologian and preacher Dr Moody would not go to sleep until he had spoken to at least one person that day about God. Yet how often we remain indifferent and lazy in carrying out God's work! I've noticed that frequently, when we gather to study the word of God, we digress into idle chatter, forgetting that our strength is based on communion with the Creator.

Valeri, which instruments do you play? Where did you learn? If you can, send a diagram of some guitar attachment or phaser. What kind of attachment is used for the guitar for playing 'The world is steeped in sin'? This song has a refrain ending in the words 'What shall I do?' with the guitar following in a very high key. Also could you explain how to play various rhythms on bass guitar? There are some I've heard of, but have no music. Although my musical training is not brilliant, I can play well enough from music, as I played the mandolin in Leningrad for two years. I'd love to meet someone from your group and must admit I miss Leningrad young people.

What do you think, are young people developing now in the direction of God, or just the opposite? We hear rumours about questionable, if not downright unchristian behaviour among some young people. I believe that worldly considerations are penetrating the hearts of

184

many of God's children. May he preserve us in purity and his light!

I hope to hear from you soon.

The following extracts are taken from two letters written by a close friend of Valeri during his military service. He knew about the plans to record *The Trumpet Call* from the beginning:

A hearty soldier's greeting to you from. . . . They took me into the army on 1st December (1982) and brought us here to the Murmansk region to the town . . . . We arrived here on the morning of 3rd December. We were taken to our units immediately, shaved, washed, given uniforms and after that were swiftly 'taken in hand': drill, early rising, punctuality, rules and regulations and all that sort of thing.

Our engineering unit isn't a very big one and we're training as sappers. The food isn't too bad, but you can never get enough. Wherever we go we have to march in formation and sing as we go. Our sergeant is quite a tough nut – has us on the hop from morning till night. Still, that's army life: we can take it. Moreover, I'm not alone here and know from whom I can expect support. There's very little time for letter writing, so I'm sorry this letter is so short and messy. Write as often as you can, even if I don't reply at once: they really work us hard. That's all for now! Write soon and give my regards to everyone.

* * * *

Thank God, I've received a long-awaited letter from you at last! I'm very glad that your work, blessed by God, has finally been completed and that Trumpet Call is taking the message of the Holy Scripture to the world. Glory to Christ! Here in the unit I've met several blokes who've also become very keen on our idea, the truth!

They're dying to hear the recording you've made, so send us one on tape (we've no cassettes here) as soon as possible, in the stereo version if you can.

Although I'm in the army, I'm not just sitting around doing nothing – I spread the word – the glad tidings – to all who wish to know God! There are some *very* good musicians here and we've formed a group and are composing on Christian themes. You can write here without worrying, but don't put your address on the envelope, or put down a fictitious one. You know yourself how the KGB operates, and it would serve no useful purpose for me to attract their attention at this stage. When I get back from army service we'll continue our common task and I'm certain (the Lord help me in this) that I shall bring a large number of people to God.

My army service is progressing well, my health is fine and I'm in absolutely marvellous spirits. I'm totally involved in my mission and burn with the desire to do as much of God's work as I can. God willing, I shall later come to Piter. Write as much as you can about yourself, about all of you, about your successes. Also, send me texts and music of good Christian songs. Well, that's about it for this time. I await the tape and a long letter with great eagerness. May the Lord bless us and our endeavours! Amen.

(signature)   30th May 1983
[Note: Illustration of a cross bursting through clouds in corner of the sheet of paper.]

Many of the believers who wrote to Valeri and Sergei understood very well the nature of their struggle with the authorities. Some had had first hand experience of persecution. Together with the many words of encouragement and exhortations to Valeri and Sergei to 'continue their work', they wrote with dismay about the unjust treatment of religious believers:

Like you, I'm a believer, but I belong to the Orthodox faith. I'm deeply disgusted by the attitude of our authorities to rock groups such as yours. I'm certain that you don't sing anti-Soviet songs, call for war, or anything of that kind. Therefore why should they forbid you to stage public concerts and subject you to surveillance? After all, there's supposed to be freedom of religion in the Soviet Union, and that means it's permitted.

We hope that Trumpet Call will soon receive permission to perform publicly in concert halls.

Best regards to your family, friends and all those who put their trust in the Almighty.

The following letter is the only one which actually expresses 'unchristian' sentiments:

Please don't take this unsolicited letter amiss. I heard about your group in a recent BBC broadcast which mentioned two addresses, one of which was yours. I'm writing to you because it's closest to where I live. I've been disgusted for a long time by many of the things taking place in our country. I'm always extremely upset when I hear about the persecution of the latest victims of the KGB. Those bastards have gone unchecked for too long. They are everywhere. Even at pop concerts. Never mind, in our part of the town we do as much as we can to get back at these vigilantes. I was very favourably impressed by your music. I have been baptised, but am only just beginning to experience official pressure because of this. Next week I'm to be visited again by an investigator. Still, I made up my mind to write to you. I'd very much like to obtain a tape of your work, but write to me first. Please write. Tell me something about your group.

Valeri also received letters from Christians who were evidently very young in the faith and not actively involved in any particular church or fellowship. Two seventeen-year-old students wrote about the frustrations of their everyday lives:

> My friend and I would like to thank you for the letter you sent us. To be quite honest, we didn't really expect any response from you because you have much more important things to worry about than letter-writing. Nevertheless, my friend . . . and I both thank you very much indeed. Today is Friday and I'm sitting beside my radio waiting for the BBC to come on the air as I write.

> I'd like to tell you something about . . . and myself. We're the same age, both seventeen, and are students at the Krasnoholmsk Agricultural Institute. We're both great fans of modern music, but it's very hard to get tapes. There's a disco in town, but even though everybody here knows everybody else, the chances of getting something for taping are nil. Everyone wants to grab something for himself, and to hell with everybody else. Therefore even though . . . and I have a tape recorder each, there's nothing to listen to on them: we're sick to death of the small amount of stuff we do have, and getting anything new is virtually impossible. So thank you again for your promise to send us tapes – that was a treat we didn't expect.

> As for your faith – we think it's great. To tell the truth, . . . and I believe in God. Of course, we don't go to pray in church or keep the fasts, we simply believe that he is there, even though these days such a thing is probably rare. In my own lifetime I've seen on many occasions that man is not brother to man, but rather to a wolf. Everything around us is now based on deceit, lies and theft. People seem unable to live any other way. How can there possibly be any genuine talk of communism? Nobody is ever going even to approach such a thing. Most probably, as God created man, he

188

will be the one to put an end to man either by another Great Flood or by war. However, I seem to be straying from the point. So here we are, living in our small town. Although it's not big, it's the regional centre, some 400 kilometres from Leningrad and 300 from Moscow. There's nothing here worth writing about apart from, perhaps, that in the centre of the town there's a 50 metre bell-tower which was built 500 years ago.

Well, that's all for now. Best regards to all the members of the group. We're waiting to hear about you. If you can, write some more about yourselves. To borrow your own words – God be with you!

Finally, among the correspondents are those who have endured direct persecution for their Christian faith. Their testimonies are the most uplifting and must have been a tremendous encouragement to Valeri and Sergei in the midst of their problems. The following quotations are from a series of five letters from a believer living in Soviet Moldavia. They provide a fascinating insight into the life of the registered Baptist Church which he attends and give an account of the attempts made by the authorities to disrupt church life:

I greet you from Moldavia, dear brothers in Christ! Peace be with you! We were very happy to hear of your great endeavour. We wish you success in this toil in the fields of the Lord! Use your God-given talents to the limit. Great are the rewards of God for those who love him and who confess him before all men. As for persecution – do not fear it. The apostle Peter instructs us to fortify ourselves with knowledge of Christ's sufferings for our sakes (1 Peter 4.1). In the Gospel of Matthew it is said: 'I send you forth like sheep among the wolves; therefore be as wise as serpents and innocent as doves' (Matt 10.16). Arm yourselves with this advice, pray to the Lord and serve him with courage. May you prosper in his work. Greetings to you also from your sister in Christ, . . . (my wife) and our two children.

May God keep you!

The next letter from the above was written on Holy Saturday, 1983:

Dear brothers, we greet you and your families! Christ is Risen! How joyful is this day of the resurrection of our Lord, a mark of our salvation and the evidence of the divinity of Christ. All glory to him, and boundless joy to us.

On Thursday and Friday we attended services with breaking of bread in memory of the death of Christ. Tomorrow, God willing, we shall attend the Sunday service. Getting to church is not too difficult – about 40 kilometres.

On 1st May some of the young brothers from the congregation held a service somewhere outside town and were apprehended by the militia on their way back. A 'paper' was made out, they were threatened, but the youngest refused to leave the militia post until everyone was released. I heard the radio programme about you, God be praised. Although there was quite a lot of jamming, I managed to hear your letter in its entirety.

I can't say I was surprised – that's typical of 'their' methods of operation. We also have psychiatrists coming round at work, or are ordered to go to them through the drafting board*, or are summoned to the KGB and 'cautioned'. Warmest regards to Valeri, how are things with him now? How good it is to know that we're in God's care and that we need fear nobody; 'What can man do unto us, when we're with God?'

* For military recruitment. The writer is a former air force officer.

How hard it must be for the unbelieving! Our church in ... is a registered one, and used to be very good, but now the authorities have forbidden the young people's choir, band and children's circle. Still, thank God, things could be worse: God's work continues, we have various groups, choirs and musicians to praise him.

It's a very good thing that your Trumpet Call group consists of representatives of different churches; it's time all Christians got together in the service of the Lord. We pray for you. May God send you strength and wisdom in serving him and spreading the word.

Don't give way to despair – but you're not doing so, in any case – continue to stand for the truth, put your gift to his service and 'stand against the Evil One, and he shall flee from you' (James 4.7). The grace of God and blessings upon you all. If the Lord should will it, we shall travel up and meet you – we'd like this very much. God be with you.

★　★　★　★

Christ is Risen! We greet you in joy. We heard about you on the radio. Praise God that you've had the glory of suffering for the name of Christ. 'All who would live in Christ shall suffer persecution' (2 Tim. 3.12). Don't fear their wrath and don't despair. But, thank God, you obviously don't fear 'them'.

At church one of our brothers preached a sermon about suffering and then read out a long list of those who are even now suffering for Christ in psychiatric hospitals, prisons, hard labour camps, places of exile, who are under arrest on trumped-up charges. There are families where the wife has been left to raise seven or more children (while the husband serves his sentence) but they don't yield to despair, they pray and fortify their faith in service to the Lord, glorifying his name. I was also forced to go to a psychiatrist by the drafting board:

191

'How can this be that you're an air force officer on the reserve – and a Baptist?' The Lord turned away the shafts of the wicked at that time. A year later the psychiatrist came to me at my place of work, saying it was time for me to go into psychiatric hospital for observation. I managed, however to stand my ground and not submit to their pressure. Now I'm trying to find another job. One factory agreed to take me on as a toolmaker, I passed the medical, but when I came to start work they set out the condition that I could work there only if I gave an undertaking that nobody at the factory should know that I was a believer. How could I possibly not witness to the Lord? He will not leave me wanting, I shall find some other job, and continue to witness.

* * * *

Christ is Risen!

On Sunday we went to church. Everything passed off quietly – by that I mean there was no sign of 'them' at the gates, although later on some 'representatives of the people' did turn up. The weather was fine, which was just as well, otherwise all of us who had to stand outside the church would have had to huddle under umbrellas. I've written to brother Valeri, but don't know whether my letter will reach him. On 6 May I was summoned by the head of the regional KGB. He showed me some letter, allegedly written by me, stating that I was renouncing my Soviet citizenship and similar rubbish and spent quite a while trying to get me to 'confess'. Then he wanted to know why it was that I have spoken in defence of arrested pastors, he abused our church and Baptists generally ('they're not engaged in the campaign for peace') and read out to me article 67 of the Moldavian criminal code (anti-Soviet agitation and propaganda) and demanded that I stop speaking about God. Then he tried to get me to sign a statement saying that I had no wish to leave the USSR, that I thought

Communists were wonderful, that I would not so much as mention God to anyone again. In exchange for this, he promised that I would immediately be given a permanent job. Naturally, I refused to have anything to do with this provocation.

On 10th May I went to sign on (I have a temporary job as a furnace stoker) while waiting to start a toolmaker's job in a factory. In the personnel department they devoted a great deal of time to my religious convictions ('Baptists want to see us all dead', and so on). Finally, the woman in charge said: 'We'll sign you up on condition that you won't tell a soul in the factory that you're a believer. Otherwise, you'll have me to deal with! We won't have you corrupting our young people.' Of course, I refused to give any such undertaking, for didn't Christ say that he would witness before the Father for those who witness for him before men, and spurn those who spurned him? After this I was sent to the section manager (the Party organiser) who said that my position had been scrapped and there was no other job they could give me.

I thanked the Lord that he had given me the strength to withstand the forces of evil. I rest secure in the knowledge that he will not leave us. This is nothing new, after all, and not the first time I've lost my job because of my faith. I've been unable to secure steady employment for more than a year now. Things are becoming more difficult, yet it's written that those who would live in the Lord shall suffer persecution (2 Tim. 3.12). Therefore, 'rejoice and be glad, for great is your reward in heaven'. This refers to all of us, in all the corners of our country and elsewhere. You, in Leningrad, will also remain in his care, and he will send you strength to evade the snares of the ungodly. From the bottom of my heart I wish you victory, health, good spirits, courage and fortitude and all that's good and bright. Greetings to all of you in the Trumpet Call, true children of God. May he preserve and keep you. Amen.

Such letters with the exhortation to endure persecution gladly for the sake of the gospel follow a worthy tradition which began with the apostle Paul writing letters from a Roman prison where he was being held for proclaiming his faith in Jesus Christ. For Valeri and Sergei the receipt of all these letters could not have been clearer evidence of the spirit of God at work.

9: Preaching to the lost youth

Valeri wrote his series of sermons as a direct response to the letters which he and Sergei had received, but thought of the sixty or so correspondents as being representative of a much wider audience. Spurred on by the effectiveness of the initial radio broadcasts from the West, he quickly realised that he had the potential to reach millions of young people throughout the Soviet Union by broadcasting his sermons over Western radio. It was impossible for him personally to follow up each individual who had been affected by his music, but he felt responsible to each one and desperately wanted somehow to communicate with them.

His aim in his sermons was to preach the gospel in a straightforward manner. His goal was to point the way to Jesus Christ as the Saviour of the world, to demonstrate the woeful inadequacy of man's sinful nature, to explain the need for repentance, to show how to live daily in the presence of Christ and most significantly, to draw attention to Christ's second coming.

In the course of his sermons he tries to answer many of the questions that were raised in the letters. Valeri does not claim to be a theologian or even an experienced Bible teacher; he is not a man of great learning – he never had the opportunity to become one – but what he does possess is first-hand experience of God working powerfully in his own life and in the lives of those around him. He draws on his own experience of God to convince people of the truth of the claims of Christianity. He urges his listeners to put God to the test, to bring their doubts and questions to God and ask him to reveal himself. He also draws on his personal knowledge of the Bible and the teaching he received at the Leningrad Baptist Church.

Christians and other religious believers in the Soviet Union are discriminated against and treated as second-class citizens. They are denied the opportunity to share and spread their faith or to make a useful contribution to society through caring ministries such as church hospitals, old people's and children's homes, hospices or any other charitable institution. To Christians who are physically abused, tortured and imprisoned for their faith, a country such as America where there is freedom of belief must, by comparison, appear to be a kind of paradise. However, Valeri does not believe that evil and injustice exist only within the Soviet system. He makes it quite clear in his sermons that the problem of man's sin is a universal one.

Some of the sermons which follow are given in full. Where I do not give the whole text, I have picked out the main themes and illustrated them with quotations. Valeri intended them to be listened to as a series. He starts in the first one on a personal note, by giving his testimony of how he became a Christian. He begins as follows:

Dear Friends,

I greet you all in the name of the Christian group, the Trumpet Call, and in the name of our Lord Jesus Christ. Recently we celebrated the great festival of the Resurrection of Christ and the wonderful words 'Christ is risen' were on the lips of every Christian. Of course, these words are in the heart of every Christian each day, not only at Easter. Twenty years ago when I was a youth before call-up age I could not say 'Christ is Risen'. No God whatsoever existed for me.

Following his testimony, Valeri's first main point is that the whole world is tainted and spoiled by the existence of evil. He refutes the Marxist view that as communist societies throughout the world gradually evolve and conditions in these societies improve men and women will become better human beings. Rather he identifies evil both as inherent sinfulness in man and as a powerful external force in the world – the devil or Satan – working in opposition to God. He personifies Satan and describes him as God's supreme enemy who keeps man in subjection, enslaves him so that the life he lives bears no resemblance to the life which God intended for his created beings and finally seeks to destroy man because he is part of God's creation made in God's image. He warns his listeners that those who are seeking higher values in life are the ones Satan will attempt most actively to destroy:

> If you see that lies and injustice rule in this world, then you will know that the ruler of this world is the devil and his aim is to swallow up honest people. Why should he wish to harm those who have already lost their integrity or those who have a stone where their hearts should be?

Valeri anticipates that many who listen to his sermon will say to themselves, 'But I don't believe in any external force, good or evil; I'm in charge of my own life – it belongs to me'. Valeri categorically refutes this idea. Because man's basic nature is sinful, according to Valeri, he is already in the clutches of Satan. The only way to break out of this condition is to turn to Christ, to repent and give one's life to him. Valeri states: 'If you don't give yourself to Jesus who loves you, then because of your sinful nature you belong to the devil.' If you're not for Christ you're a slave of the devil. There is no middle way.

He enumerates four ways in which the devil tries to ensnare and destroy people. Having earlier described his personal struggle and moments of total despair when he was in the army before he became a Christian, he claims that one of the devil's methods is to drive people to the point of taking their own life:

> I myself realised that life was not a fairy tale. Rather it's a circle of lies, hypocrisy, evil and injustice. It's

senseless trying to struggle out of it. You're in a vicious circle. This godless mechanism twisted me, it was simply impossible to withstand it and therefore I decided the only resort was to commit suicide.

The second way the devil offers is for you simply to let life take its course, gradually become addicted to drink and go to seed. Look around you and you'll find plenty of people like this. Thirdly if you are a serious-minded person and you have a family and friends, well, as the saying goes, if you want to live you've got to know how to fiddle – make up a few lies here, hush up something there. The fourth way is to violate your own conscience and the spirit of comradeship and then the king of sinners, the ruler of the world, the devil, will say to you: 'I will give you everything, money, fame. . .'. But if you choose this way you join the category of people described in the proverb: 'Dirt always comes to the surface, but after all, no one sees your black soul underneath your white shirt and tie'. Dear friends, if you still have powers of reasoning, if you still want to live and live eternally, then choose God's way. Christ said: 'I am the way, the truth and the life'. Why be a slave to sin? Christ gave you freedom on the cross at Golgotha. Accept his sacrifice and give yourself to God and you will be restored to a new life by the power of the Risen Christ. Then you will joyfully extol him with the words, 'Christ is risen indeed'.

Having laid the foundation for a basic understanding of Christianity, Valeri, in his second sermon, discusses some very important questions – the nature of the Church, the Trinity, Christian unity, the uniqueness of Christianity compared with other world religions and the availability of the Bible in the Soviet Union. He starts by explaining how God revealed himself as one God to mankind before the coming of Christ by choosing the nation of Israel to be His people:

God chose Israel, abundantly blessed his people and did works and miracles, so that the whole world would understand that he is the one living God. In order that the Israelites could continually receive God's blessing, he appointed prophets and priests from among them and through them he gave specific teaching, decrees and laws. When we read the Old Testament starting with the five books of Moses and going on to the birth of Christ in the New Testament, we see that all the prophets bore testimony to the coming of the Messiah, the Christ. Who then was this Christ and what was his purpose on earth? Well, first of all we shall look at the first book of the prophet Moses, Genesis. God appeared (revealed himself) in many different ways. In the third chapter, verse twenty-two, we read the following: 'And the Lord God said, behold the man is become as one of Us.' Think about that phrase, 'one of Us'. The word 'us' is written with a capital letter.

In John's Gospel in the first chapter we read: 'In the beginning was the Word and the Word was with God and the Word was God'. In the fourteenth verse of this chapter we read: 'And the Word was made flesh and dwelt among us, full of grace and truth'. Pay attention to this phrase, 'and the Word became flesh'.

We know that God is a spiritual moving force and it is not possible to see him with our physical eyes, but God came and took on human form through the blessed Virgin Mary and through this great mystery the Lord God reveals himself to us in two forms – as the Father Creator of all that is visible and invisible and as the Son of God. And the aim of Jesus' coming to this sinful world was to die for the sins of the whole world, to reconcile through his sacrifice all sinners with the heavenly Father, to be a perfect example of holiness for all his followers, to rise again from the dead by the power of Almighty God and to reveal the third part of the Godhead – the Holy Spirit. But the latter is given only to those who give themselves completely to God. And so we see the New Testament reveals for us one God in three persons: Father, Son and Holy Spirit.

In order to understand the triune God, let's look at God's likeness – mankind. Man is also three in one, body, soul and spirit. But we won't diverge from our theme, we must continue. God chose Israel and Jesus came to them in the flesh. We read in the Gospel of John that 'Christ came to his own and his own knew him not. But to those who knew God he gave power to become sons of God' (John 1.11–12). So Christ came into the world and left behind him his church.

Here, of course, you will raise an objection. The one Church which we see here on earth has been spoiled, especially in our day. Where is its unity? Let's start at the beginning again. In my last sermon I talked about the fact that the ruler of this world is the devil and therefore any movement, even a religious one, which appears here on earth will never be perfect, because the devil destroys everything that is good and beautiful even if people don't believe in his existence.

Let's take the example of our communist party. It was founded by so many outstanding people who were willing to make personal sacrifices. The word 'communist' was spoken with pride. But because of man's sin the devil got to work in this party to such an extent that now if you call someone a communist, in the majority of cases, it has a completely negative connotation. It means that such a person is either a hypocrite or a black marketeer, operating on a huge scale. Our major newspapers constantly bear witness to this fact. At best the person is a time-server, counting on receiving privileges.

Various religious movements are subject, in exactly the same way, to attacks from the devil, but they don't succumb as quickly as the atheist ones. The devil has to struggle very hard with believers. Only the one Church of Christ remains absolutely inaccessible to the devil. You ask what exactly is this church, the one Church of Christ. It's the sum total of all those Christians who belong, in the first place, to Jesus Christ and not to any religious movement. It's not important which denomination they belong to – Orthodox, Catholic, Baptist – what's important is that they are Christians. If they are, there can be no quarrels or divisions. It's important to understand that any religious movement is like a religious organisation here on earth whose aim is to teach men to live in close contact with God through Jesus Christ. To teach them to be led, to walk with God daily through the Holy Spirit.

A religious movement is only the beginning for Christians: it's the means by which they are perfected, but they all join the ranks of the one Church, which is a living organism. In the one Church of Christ, Christians are guided not by people, but by the leading of the Holy Spirit and they base their learning not on religious literature, but on the Bible.

I want to say a few words about the Bible. This book was inspired by God himself through his chosen people and consists of two parts, the Old and the New Testaments. It's a catalogue of life. It's the basic source of teaching for the Christian and every Christian should read it every day in order not to go astray or to become distant from God. In John's Gospel (5.39) Christ said: 'You search the scriptures because you think that in them you have eternal life, and it is they that bear witness to me'.

I want to quote two verses, the first from 2 Timothy 3.16: 'All scripture is inspired by God and profitable for teaching, for reproof, for correction and for training in righteousness that the man of God may be complete, equipped for every good work.' The second is from 1

Timothy 4.16: 'Take heed to yourself and to your teaching; hold to that, for by doing so you will save both yourself and your hearers'.

But where can I get a Bible, you ask? Yes, the shortage of Bibles in our country is a big problem. About five months ago, when I was summoned to see an official at the CRA in connection with our rock group, the Trumpet Call, we had a conversation about the Bible in the presence of a KGB officer. I told the official that the government policy towards us believers was a senseless one. For example they should issue as many Bibles as are needed to meet the demand among believers because the majority of them have never even seen a Bible. I told them that if they produced ten million copies of the Bible they would be snatched up in a second and even that number would not be sufficient because there's a spiritual awakening throughout our country, especially among young people.

I explained that because of the shortage of Bibles active Christians have to set up secret printing presses, to establish links with Western Christian organisations and the government has to waste huge sums of money searching for these secret presses and keeping Christians under surveillance (unnecessarily). And then we read about these Christians in the newspapers – these dregs of society, these cowards who print anti-Soviet literature. How can they be cowards when the activities they're engaged in demonstrate that they're brave and unselfish? How can they be the dregs of society when they're working for their own people motivated by the love of Christ? The Bibles which they produce at grave risk are distributed free of charge. Inside each copy you'll find the words 'not for resale'.

The CRA official replied: 'You must understand, we simply don't have enough paper – in our country paper is in short supply'. Then I suggested that the government should talk to Western Christian organisations who would provide as many Bibles as are needed free of charge. 'Why is it necessary to make a fuss in the West so they find out about our paper shortage?' And he immediately changed the subject.

I've thought about this problem a great deal and can't help reminding myself of the fact that when our country is short of grain for breadmaking it gets huge supplies from the West. The Bible is heavenly bread for mankind. It is written, 'Man shall not live by bread alone, but by every word which proceeds from the mouth of God'. So what can I advise you, my friends, if you want a Bible? This is not a problem for God. Christ said, 'Whatever you ask for in my name it will be given – only believe.' So then turn to him and he will arrange everything so that you will receive one.

Let me conclude by giving a summary – there is one God, one channel between God and man – Christ; one book of knowledge – the Bible, and one Church which the Lord is preparing in these last days before his glorious return to take all believers to be with him in his eternal kingdom. Christ is near.

In his third sermon, Valeri describes the sanctifying work of the Holy Spirit in the life of a believer and how this enables the believer to fulfil Christ's commandment to his disciples to go and preach the gospel to the whole world:

Dear Friends,
I greet you in the name of the Christian rock group, Trumpet Call, in the name of our Lord Jesus Christ. Today we're going to talk about the mission of the Christian. First of all, what is a Christian? A Christian is someone whose heart is ruled by unselfish love. The aim of the Christian is to spread the gospel, the joyful news of salvation to everyone around him. In other

words, to point out that Jesus died for our sins, that Jesus calls not the righteous, but sinners to repentence, that Jesus changes the life of every human being who draws near to him. And Christ himself says in the Gospel, 'Who wants to follow me must forget himself.' In other words, not to live for self, but for others. Take up your cross, in other words, witness to the truth, do not turn back, follow me. He leads us along a difficult path in life, but a pure and wonderful one. Each one of us knows that to live for others is to be fulfilled. A Christian should work, not out of a sense of duty, because Christ does not force or constrain anyone, but out of a sense of love which dwells in the heart of every genuine Christian. This kind of love is described in the words of the following poem:

Love is gentle, not haughty.
Love is pure, it contains no deviousness or guile.
Love is dependable, truthful,
selfless and upright.
Love is patient, full of forgiveness and forbearance.
Love endures all things.
Love does not dwell on evil, does not judge.
Love never fails.

How can such perfect love, the love of Christ, be enthroned in our hearts? Only by giving ourselves completely to Jesus – this is the only condition which God presents to us. He says to us 'Come to me, all who labour and are heavy laden, and I will give you rest.' In Psalm 37 we read the following: 'Commit your way to the Lord, trust in Him and He will act'. In other words, if we do not give ourselves to God, because of our sinful nature we belong to the devil.

So often we come across people who believe in God, in the saving power of Christ, who have read a great deal of spiritual literature, but who have not given themselves to him. It's as if they find themselves next to

Christ, but not in Christ. But if a person sincerely prays, saying, 'Into your hands Lord, I give my whole life. Take me from this moment as a future child and lead me through life according to your will' – then Christ, by his Holy Spirit, will enter the heart of that person. 'And the Spirit of God himself will bear witness to our spirit, that we are children of God.' And although formerly we were born of the flesh and we came from human parents, from that moment we are born of God into a new, holy and pure life. (Christ said: 'I will not leave you desolate; I will come to you (John 14.18).)

Now I want you to note something else. No one from any of those religious movements which reject Christ as the Messiah can be adopted by God, unless he accepts Christ Jesus as the sacrifice for his sins which separate him from God. Of course, the Lord always helps those who truly call on him. But that does not mean that he makes them his children. People spend so much time and expend so much effort trying to perfect themselves spiritually, but they will never achieve it. We can perfect ourselves only if we become children of God because then Christ becomes our strength.

When we are reborn as children of God, through us he can heal the sick, drive out demons and perform miracles. But in order to do these things we have to know and do the will of God.

The fact that we were able to form the Christian rock group Trumpet Call in an atheist country is, in itself, a great miracle.

So, a Christian is a person regenerated by God. What is his mission here on earth? Jesus himself said it clearly in few words: 'Go into the whole world and preach the gospel'. In other words go and tell everyone about Jesus. Tell them how he has forgiven you and adopted you as his child. Tell them about how he answers your prayers and helps you when you are in difficulties. Tell them what the Lord God has done for you.

I remember when I started to witness to the truth I found it very difficult, because I knew so little about God. But I knew the main things and I concentrated on the fact that Christ was my saviour, that the heavenly Father who adopted me as a son was all-powerful and full of love. I gave many examples of how he had helped me. Sometimes in the course of a conversation I found myself in difficulties and I immediately referred to my Christian aunt and said, 'If you talk to my aunt she'll be able to answer all your questions'. But perhaps you think that only experienced Christians, really holy people, should preach the gospel to those around them and that you must first of all achieve this level of holiness. But let me ask you something. What is holiness? A holy person is one who has given himself to Christ, a regenerated person whose heart is filled with love for all mankind. In the first letter of Peter (2.10) we read the following: 'Once you were no people, but now you are God's people; once you had not received mercy, but now you have received mercy'.

I'm reminded of the story of Lazarus. Christ raised Lazarus from the dead and Lazarus came out of the tomb still wrapped in a shroud. Jesus said: 'Unbind him'. Or in other words, take away the grave clothes. In the same way, Christ gives new life to those who are dead in sin. Our hearts become pure and holy because the Holy Spirit dwells in them. If the core of our being is holy, then everything else will be made whole and a time will come when Christ will take from us the shroud of sin. Day by day the Christian is being transformed by actively working in God's harvest field. In John 15.2 we read that if we bear spiritual fruit the heavenly Father will refine us, so that we may bear more fruit.

I shall never forget that when I gave my life to the Lord

I received such joy because the Holy Spirit overflowed in my heart and I simply had to share this with others. And at that moment it was as if the Lord prompted me and said to me – 'Go back to the place I have brought you from, to the terrible place where your friends are perishing. Let them see in you the joy of salvation which I have given you. Tell them that I in my power will save them too, if they call upon my name. Go to them. They are your friends. You know exactly what kind of people they are. You know which key may unlock the door of their hearts. Do everything in your power at least to make them pause and think and not to perish. I will bless you, I so long for them to be saved. But when you go back to your old environment, don't get mixed up in it, on the contrary be like salt and light because I am with you'.

And so, my friends, go forward and work in God's harvest. And in order to radiate the love of God to others keep closely in touch with him through prayer. Read the Bible every day. Work for six days, but remember that the seventh is a day sanctified by God. Go at least once a week to God's house because this is a specially sacred place, filled with the presence of God, where he is able to bless us for the week ahead and where, through his chosen servants, he reveals to us the truth from his word. But when you leave the church you must once again begin the struggle against the dark and evil forces of atheism which ravage the human spirit and cause people to fill the emptiness in their lives with alcohol, drugs, vanity or riches, or causes them to abandon life altogether. In conclusion I will read a verse from a collection of spiritual songs:

Life is given to us to love,
to love limitlessly, unceasingly,
and to dedicate to all those who suffer
our minds, our bodies our life-blood.

Life is given to us
to comfort those who are outcasts,
[those who are] oppressed,
to offer warmth and to take upon ourselves
the needs and sorrows of the afflicted.

Life is given to us
to struggle endlessly
against darkness and lies
and to sow the seed of the holy truth of God
in the hearts of our brothers.

For it is by loving
and offering our love unstintingly
we dedicate to those who suffer
our minds, our bodies and our lifeblood.

In his fourth sermon, Valeri tells his listeners how
important it is to encourage one another by sharing what
God has done in and through them. He gives a very
moving example of how God enabled him to preach the
gospel to a group of teenagers in a juvenile prison. He
introduces this anecdote by talking about God as a God
of miracles in our day:

You know, sometimes when a preacher preaches about
the miracles recorded in the Bible performed by the
prophets, Jesus and by the saints, one has the
impression that those miracles were for that time and
such miracles do not happen today. But if a preacher
speaks about a miracle which God has performed
through him personally, then I for one am filled with
zeal and I think to myself, if God can show his strength
through a preacher, he can show his heavenly power
through me, too. I want you to understand that a
preacher who speaks about how God has helped him
personally in his work in God's harvest, and has shown
him miracles and acts of healing, has a far greater effect
on the hearts of his listeners than a preacher who

preaches a theoretical sermon. Now I want to tell you how God helped me.

In the summer of 1972 when I was working at the motor vehicle depot in Leningrad at Trinity Fields I had to transport a lorryload of wooden planks to the juvenile prison at Kolpinsky. I felt that God was sending me to this place and I prayerfully prepared myself for preaching the gospel, aware of the great responsibility placed on me by the Almighty. I knew that this might be my only opportunity and, conscious of my own weakness, I called on God and asked him to arrange the circumstances so that the light of the gospel would be revealed to these young hearts in the juvenile prison. I prayed at work without anyone else knowing what I was doing and I tried to keep up my prayer contact without interruption. Whether I was at home or at the transport depot I had to be constantly close to God, bringing my needs before him or simply rejoicing in him.

I drove into the prison zone, parked the lorry at the unloading bay and a group of young prisoners approached me, so I had to think fast. I had only a few seconds and I prayed. Suddenly I noticed the prison guard walking away from the group. 'Now' I thought to myself, 'better get started.'

I climbed up onto a high stack of wooden planks and shouted out 'Hey, lads, come here a minute!' They surrounded me with puzzled stares – there were about thirty of them. 'Lads', I said, 'You can ask me whatever you like about God, about life. I'm a believer and I can talk to you about these things.' A friendly conversation started up. I tried to talk about the essential things in a simple way that they would understand.

But then the prison guard returned and was surprised to see me standing on the top of this hugh pile, talking about God quite openly. He started to question me. The lads followed the conversation with great interest and it soon became obvious that they were on my side. When he realised that in defending his atheist views he was being made to look stupid, he sloped off. I knew that he would bring one of the high-ups back with him, so I quickly concluded my conversation with these young offenders. I told them that if they seriously thought over what I had said and offered themselves, and their violent and unruly natures to God, if they repented and placed themselves in his hands they would, through the power of Christ, become great workers and evangelists.

Just as I had finished I heard a shout: 'Hey you, come here'. The shout came from the prison governor who was just approaching. I went up to him and he said: 'What kind of propaganda are you spreading here?' 'Comrade governor, I'm not spreading propaganda, I'm simply doing some educational work with your inmates. You're concerned that they should become good citizens and I've been telling them about Christ, because only Christ can re-educate sinners – every sinner must come to him.' The prison governor was clearly taken aback by my reply. Then this man, whom the state had trusted to re-educate these young delinquents, let out a stream of violent, unrepeatable abuse. The clear indication was that I should get out before it was too late.

I got into my lorry which had been unloaded, but just as I was setting off I noticed a good-looking lad of about twelve who had hidden himself behind the stack of planks. He was staring at me and then he called out: 'Hey, mate – how do you pray?' I told him that God wasn't interested in empty words, nor automatic gestures or rituals, but what is in a person's heart. 'Call on him and the heavenly Father will help you through any difficulty'.

I left the prison zone with a feeling of exaltation. I thanked God that he had helped me to preach to the lads and thought to myself that probably the Almighty had sent me primarily to that young boy. Perhaps his own mother had been praying for him and God had heard her.

The next morning at the depot they told me I had to go to the prison again. On the way I called at home and grabbed an old copy of Luke's Gospel in the hope that I would be able to give it to the boy. As I hadn't eaten anything that morning, I decided not to eat at all from that moment until I returned from the juvenile prison, having won a spiritual victory. In other words, I decided to fast. Fasting is a form of urgent, purposeful prayer.

I drove in to the prison zone and there I met the same boy. I had just handed him the copy of the Gospel when one of the prison officials appeared. He was a senior lieutenant in rank. He had seen the boy throwing the Gospel underneath the lorry in order to hide it. He picked up the Gospel and took it to the prison governor. Again he let out a stream of abuse. From his empty, blustering speech, punctuated with the most terrible oaths, I gathered that he was accusing me of coming to the prison in order to spread propaganda. He said that I had already been warned once, but now I had even brought anti-Soviet literature with me (he meant the Gospel). Finally he sat down at a table and began to prepare some documentation about me. 'Well', I thought to myself, 'this is goodbye to my wife and kids'. But in my heart there was a deep joy and I vividly sensed the presence of the Holy Spirit.

Suddenly a prison instructor burst into the office and demanded, 'Where is the Christian?' (By this time word had got round the prison about my visit the previous day.) Then a lively conversation started up between myself and the instructor who seemed genuinely to want to discuss Christianity with me. The governor simply could not stand it. 'Shut him up', he yelled. I smiled because I felt I had won a victory. The governor saw my smile and commented maliciously, 'Let's see how you'll smile after this.' He finished what he was writing and then accompanied me to the lorry himself to ensure that I didn't talk to anyone else about God on the way.

As we approached the lorry I saw that the Lord had given me a way out of the situation. Two of the tyres on the lorry had been punctured, the petrol cap had been broken and part of the ignition system torn out. Turning to the prison governor, I said, 'Why won't you let me preach to the lads about God in order to help with their re-education? You say you're carrying out a programme of reform, but look here – I came to you in a lorry owned by the state and your lads have wrecked it. What kind of reform is that? I'll have to leave the lorry here and take this up with my boss at the transport depot'.

This was my victory, this was just what was needed. I knew that he would do anything to avoid getting a black mark for his running of the prison. He started jumping around and trying to persuade me not to ring my boss and assured me that the lorry would be quickly repaired. Of course, as a Christian, I feel sorry for people who lose their human dignity in order to save themselves and their Party membership card. I agreed to wait while they repaired the lorry. Some time later as I was driving out through the prison gates I saw the prison governor gesticulating and waving his great clenched fists and uttering curses the like of which I had never heard in my life. I knew that if I ever went there again he would simply turn me away at the prison gate. As I returned to the depot I rejoiced in the fact that the Lord had performed a miracle that very day.

I want you to know, dear friends, that God wants to

use *you* too for his glory. If you give yourself to him and serve him in these last days he will give you an abundant measure of his Holy Spirit. He will personally instruct those who respond to His call. In the scripture we read that we, God's children, have no need to fear, for the Holy Spirit will be our teacher. May God bless our new life as we wait for his glorious and imminent return. In conclusion, I will read some of Jesus' words recorded in Luke's Gospel chapter 10 verses 19–20: 'Behold, I have given you authority to tread upon serpents and scorpions and over all the power of the enemy, and nothing shall hurt you. Nevertheless, do not rejoice in this, that the spirits are subject to you; but rejoice that your names are written in heaven.' (Christ is coming soon.)

What do evangelicals in the Soviet Union think about the second coming of Christ? Those who have endured great suffering, harassment, imprisonment, physical abuse and psychiatric treatment long for his coming because they regard this as the time when their earthly sufferings will cease.

There is a strong escapist element in the faith of Soviet Evangelicals, because invariably their material situation is miserable. I have not witnessed the same intensity of emotion being expressed towards God by believers anywhere I have travelled, except perhaps in East Africa where, similarly, African Christians are not distracted by material prosperity. Soviet Evangelicals demonstrate a fervent love of God in their prayer and singing and in the way they talk about God. Their worship is often accompanied by weeping and sobbing. I believe they do have a depth of love for Christ which makes them long to see him return in all his glory far more than is the case among Christians in affluent Western societies.

An integral part of Valeri's rock opera is his message about the second coming of Christ – a warning to people to be prepared. Not unnaturally, this theme is one which Valeri writes about in some detail. He interprets very literally some passages from the book of Daniel and the book of Revelation. One may agree or disagree with his interpretations, but as it is a subject of great importance to Valeri, and indeed to many Soviet believers, this controversial subject cannot be excluded from the chapter, as it is central to Valeri's thought. It is important to bear in mind that Valeri has a limited concept of the world beyond the boundaries of the Soviet Union. Firstly what does Valeri say about the message of the Trumpet Call? The following extract is from his fifth sermon:

I want to tell you, dear friends, that the aim of our Christian rock group, Trumpet Call, brought into being by God himself, is to sound out to everyone the message of the end of the age and the second coming of our Lord Jesus Christ. Christ is coming for whom? For his Church, for those who are waiting for him, who belong to him, whether Orthodox, Catholic, Baptist, Pentecostal or Lutheran. He is also coming for those who listen to the gentle trumpet of Jesus – who, because of their sinful natures, got caught up in the snares of the devil, whether rulers, servants or workers, but who have given themselves in repentance to the Saviour. In other words, we must not be like obstinate goats who go recklessly to destruction, but like harmless sheep. Such lost sheep are gathered by the Lord through his servants and form one flock and Christ is their one good shepherd. It's not important which church you go to, you're simply required to go to God's house, but it's important to love God with all your heart, all of your soul and all your strength and to praise him for his goodness in these last days.

The second quotation is from his final sermon:

Look, even non-believers know that the whole world is sitting on a powder keg. There is terrible pollution of the atmosphere and the oceans of the world which surround all of us. Everywhere there is mistrust of the

214

authorities, strikes, works to rule, the growth of crime, inflation, unemployment. It's as if the whole world is getting ready for an unavoidable universal catastrophe. The destruction is coming from the ranks of the ungodly. So you ask, What can we do? Friends, stop in the midst of this bustle. Come to your senses. Analyse everything for and against and go to churches of different Christian confessions where they preach Christ crucified, resurrected and the Christ who is coming. Christ will adopt you if you give yourself to him completely and if you sincerely repent. Value the time that is left. Very soon the angel will take the sixth seal and after a mighty shock of the heavenly powers, a great awakening will take place and the Lord will come.

What is Valeri's attitude to the Soviet government? He says many times in the course of various letters and documents that he has no enemies. He continually stresses the importance of showing love to one's fellow man. Many eye-witnesses have seen Valeri demonstrating love to those around him. Tanya said of him: 'He's the kind of person who would take his last shirt off his own back to give to someone in need'. What provokes anger – anger which is almost tangible in his writings and spoken messages – is a system which deprives people of the right to express their religious convictions freely, which crushes their spirit, which indoctrinates them with atheism, which tries to prevent them from becoming what God intends human beings to be – adopted children, co-heirs, redeemed people. The Soviet authorities deny the existence of God and, in Valeri's view, use their propaganda to raise man to the position of a god, capable of becoming perfect and achieving total control of his environment. At the same time they keep whole nations captive by a vast network of control through the army and secret police. This, in Valeri's view, is an evil system and the Soviet policy towards religion an evil policy because it sets itself up against God. Valeri believes that both the harlot and the great city described in chapter 17 of Revelation represent the Soviet government:

In 1971 I was working in the car depot in Kherson Street in Leningrad where I came in contact with people of high rank. Naturally I talked to them about my convictions, about my beloved Saviour Jesus. I remember clearly one sentence spoken by a high Party official. He said quite openly, in a fit of temper because he couldn't find any way of opposing my witness to the truth, 'Yes, we would have wiped you believers off the face of the earth long ago, but unfortunately we can't, because we have to build socialism throughout the world'.

That sentence has been etched in my memory ever since. I've thought a great deal about it. Now in Chapter 17 of Revelation I recognise our own government. Of course, I'm not an enemy of our government, even less of our people who have endured so much suffering. The aim of this sermon is simply this, to tell everyone straight out, without hypocrisy, that to live without God is to be blind and if the blind lead the blind then both will go to perdition. God does not want sinners to perish; he wants everyone to be saved. . . . By the way, even the official at the CRA said to me that a real communist is first and foremost a godless person. And because of this, it's necessary to carry out an ideological battle against religion. . . .

Valeri draws an analogy between the building of the Tower of Babel described in the book of Genesis and the building of socialism:

Look at verse 6 of chapter 17 of Revelation which speaks of the persecution by the Kremlin government of our best people. 'I saw the woman drunk with the blood of the saints and the blood of the martyrs of Jesus; when I saw her I marvelled greatly.' Look at the

216

fifth verse: 'And on her forehead was written a name of mystery, Babylon the Great, mother of harlots and of the earth's abominations'. This means that everything which relates to Babylon relates also to our Kremlin.

Remember the tower of Babel which they wanted to build up to heaven, wishing to exalt, not God, but their own name. They built it in vain, because it served no purpose whatsoever. They chose slaves, gave them bread and water so that they did not die of starvation and said, 'Build us a name'. Isn't that just like our situation? The Kremlin, consisting of millionaires, has made us a nation of slaves, continually promising to give us a better life. To us, the slaves, they say 'You're earning too much, we'll have to cut down your wages. Build our name, long may it live'.*

In his final sermon Valeri again refers to this analogy:

Babylon is the prototype of our atheist state. We compared the tower of Babel of those times with the tower of Babel of our times. Such a coincidence is striking. It was not possible to build such a tower in those days and so we see that our people have lost faith in building this tower. They have already long ago stopped shouting: 'Long live socialism'.

Here he has chosen an image which is used frequently in Baptist preaching. In his book, *Religious Ferment in Russia*, Michael Bourdeaux quotes a poem written by a Reform Baptist which attempts to put the Soviet Union's scientific achievement into the context of man's spiritual development. The following are two verses:

> In your selfishness you scorned the Creator,
> You did not find him in the stratosphere,

* Everywhere you go in the Soviet Union you see slogans on billboards, 'Long live. . .'.

You returned to earth victoriously like God,
Robbing him of his glory.

You are firmly resolved, as in past ages,
To make your name immortal,
And have you forgotten the Tower of Babel
In your senseless struggle with God, ...

Valeri's interpretation of Revelation forms only a relatively small part of his 'theological' writing and thinking. The clear message about the second coming of Christ in the rock musical is set firmly in the context of a call to repentance and recognition of the redemptive work of Christ on the cross.

10: Prisoner for God

1983 was a year of great anxiety and physical and emotional suffering, but also of spiritual victory. With Valeri's release from psychiatric hospital and the impact this had on members of the Leningrad Church as well as his friends and followers, the year had ended on a note of triumph.

Many of Valeri's friends in Western Europe and America had lived through these traumas with Valeri, albeit at a safe distance, and identified with him through prayer and acts of solidarity. At the beginning of 1984 all we could do was to brace ourselves and hope that things would quieten down. But inevitably the question of what the authorities would do next was uppermost in our minds.

The fiasco over the psychiatric internment had been embarrassing to them and it had given rise to a great deal of adverse publicity in the West. But Valeri had already been warned early in 1983 that a criminal case was being prepared against him. The doctors at the psychiatric hospital had said openly that if it proved impossible to convict Valeri on a criminal charge, they could simply declare him insane and this would be an effective way of disposing of him. This was clearly the authorities' intention from the beginning. It was simply a question of time and finding just the right pretext.

Why was Valeri such an irritant? There were a number of reasons. Firstly he was an evangelist and had had considerable success in drawing young people to the Christian faith and to church. This success was partly due to the fact that he used rock music as a medium to persuade

219

young people to listen to his message. The authorities' disquiet about the impact of rock music has already been indicated. The fact that Valeri combined Christianity and rock music was abhorrent to them. Naturally they strongly disapproved of Valeri's contacts with Western Christians, both individuals and organisations, and the fact that he had passed on information to Western agencies.

The Soviet government is continually waging a propaganda war against Western radio broadcasting to the Soviet Union. It is estimated that more than 15 million people in the Soviet Union regularly listen to Radio Liberty broadcasts and even more than that number listen to the BBC. The authorities spend billions of roubles every year trying to jam the air waves. They have a measure of success, but they cannot wipe out this 'subversive' influence completely. The publication of numerous newspaper articles attacking Western radio programmes is another part of their offensive against 'harmful influences' from abroad. Lurid posters depicting 'unsavoury elements' such as Jews, priests and black marketeers bowing down before radio receivers which are churning out 'lies, fabrications and slander' are on sale in book shops and prominently displayed in schools and institutes of higher education. No opportunity is missed to decry publicly, in the form of lectures and speeches, the 'cursed' influence of these radio broadcasts. Unfortunately for the authorities this type of propaganda is not effective, particularly as far as young people are concerned. They simply want to hear about the latest pop scene in the West, tape the chart hits from the radio and swop recordings with their friends.

An interesting example of this type of Soviet propaganda appeared on 16th September 1984 in the Soviet newspaper targeted at young people, *Komsomolskaya Pravda*, in the form of an article entitled 'Swashbucklers of rock'n'roll'. The author, Yu. Filinov, begins by citing how, in the past, modern music has been used to good effect by the Americans as an ideological weapon:

Modern variety music has become an integral part of the spiritual life of young people. In an era of information explosion and of supersonic speeds, it reaches practically every kind of audience. Young people are attracted to it. Naturally, those who regard our country through a prism of hostility and hatred could not resist making use of this phenomenon.

Some curious, thought-provoking material was published recently in *Der Spiegel*. According to this, popular American songs and broadway shows of the thirties and forties were a proven way for the American secret services to demoralise the population of Germany during the Second World War. Translated into German and with new musical arrangements, they were relayed by the broadcasters of the secret services in order to instil into the consciousness of the opponent the basic tenets of the American way of life, to lower their will for opposition, to get rid of negative feelings towards the enemy country.

In the summer of 1944, every week eight records in German were released with popular songs and numbers from Broadway shows. This job was done in great secrecy and, as a rule, ignoring American copyright laws. The composers and authors of the texts were not put in the picture. The musicians were chosen without the knowledge of the relevant unions.

What Filinov fails to mention is the fact that at the same time as popular American tunes were being broadcast to Germany, the impact of American jazz in the Soviet Union was growing as never before and, furthermore, was fully approved of by the country's leaders. I quote from Starr's book:

The wartime alliance between the United States and the Soviet Union provided the single most important boost Soviet jazz had ever received. Without rolling back the nationalism in music, it meant that, for the time being, jazziness was no longer a sin. The recording of literally dozens of American tunes by Soviet *dzhazes* (jazz bands) caused anxiety among some of the puritans, but most saw it as fully compatible with the national effort. The official hostility to American popular culture that arose in the Soviet Union after 1946 was, in part, a reaction to the breakdown of the wartime alliance.

However, it was obviously not in Filinov's interest to take these facts into account and, having made what was intended to be an impressive historical point, he returns to the present:

And now when an aggressive American propaganda war is being waged against our socialist countries these methods remain current. The following is an extract from just one document published by a special organ of NATO, the Youth Council.

'Special attention at the present time should be paid to young people who have not had much experience of life, who are receptive to everything new, unusual, colourful and striking in the material and technical sense. Our task is to attract the young people of the USSR to the ideals of the West.'

Modern music was needed in this area because it has no boundaries or language barriers. The 'commodity' which is not subject to any customs inspection or duty has become the front runner in the ideological war. Having seen how much young people are attracted to rock music, the Western 'cooks' from the 'ideas kitchen' have concocted a menu called rock culture, especially highlighting propaganda about an independent and aggressive way of life which, apparently, is character-istic of only one category of people – the young.

Predictably, Seva Novgorodtsev of the BBC, who was

largely responsible for broadcasting extracts of Valeri's music to the Soviet Union, comes in for severe criticism. Filinov scathingly describes what a Soviet music lover might hear if he switched on the radio and happened to tune into one of the leading Western pop programmes. He attributes the following to Seva:

> Today there are dozens of groups being set up on rock'n'roll lines. But the Black Sabbatarians [this is a reference to the English group Black Sabbath] will not give up. As before, metal seethes in their furnaces, the lining has not been cracked in their crucibles and their musical converters and bessemers still smelt deafening sheaves of musical sparks. We feel sorry for the veterans of rock metallurgy because life has shown graphically that humanity needs heavy metal.

The author then refers to an article published in *Rovesnik* (*The Contemporary*) which condemned Seva as a traitor to his country. Interestingly enough, this was the article referred to by one of Valeri's correspondents (quoted on p. 169). Far from being shocked or dismayed, this young man became an instant fan of Seva after reading the article. Filinov continues:

> The head of the programme 'for young listeners in the Soviet Union who adore rock and pop music', Seva Novgorodtsev, of the BBC Russian service, gives information on 'Heavy Metal' – a type of Western popular music characterised by pathological aggressiveness and primitivism in the way in which it is performed.

> There is no need to say anything further about this person who betrayed his mother country.* The journal *Rovesnik* has disclosed it all vividly in an article entitled 'What sort of man is he?' in issue No. 9, 1982. This renegade tries with all his might to foist on his listeners

---

* In fact Seva emigrated from the Soviet Union legally in 1977.

antagonistic aesthetic tastes and doubts concerning the existence of moral norms. Gradually a certain stereotyped view insinuates itself into the perception of the listener. 'Only *we* have music which will satisfy you young people. It's only the West which brings progress to the whole of humanity. *They* don't understand you over there, but *we* do'.

Don't let's forget that the Western radio broadcasters in general are aiming to earn their Judas silver by flattering their listeners, even fawning on them. Their manner is one of dashing, familiar matiness, of trusting familiarity. Such are their methods of insinuating themselves into the confidence of young people. All this, of course, is spiced with good doses of slander.

This vituperative style betrays a sense of frustration which indicates that these 'subversive' Western broadcasts are hitting home. The author has to admit that some young people succumb to such 'propaganda':

Unfortunately, sometimes these broadcasts achieve their aim. A young person who's not yet formed his outlook on life or music listens to them and declares: 'Only rock music is worthwhile, all the rest should be thrown on the rubbish heap'. What's this – 'all the rest'? Our national heritage, classical music and the songs which our fathers and grandfathers sang as they fought and raised our country from ruins. . . .

Man is approaching spiritual poverty. Such, in fact, is the aim of the musical programmes on Western broadcasting stations. Today, on the air, you can hear songs like 'Reds in my bed' by the English group 10cc, 'Young and Russian' by the Korgis, in which they relate spine-chilling stories about notorious machinations by Moscow in the free Western world. . . .

Together with the songs, one hears statements of the

224

following type: 'We want people to be able to dance to our music even when the bombs are falling' (Simon le Bon, member of the English quintet, Duran Duran). The basic tenets of Western propaganda are spreading not only the 'cult of the sweet life', but also complete social and political indifference to the most acute problems of our time. However, more recently this bravado, this so-called absolutely apolitical approach, is being replaced by anti-communist attacks. . . .

Despite his apparent abhorrence of rock music in general – and many Western Christians would share his views on Heavy Metal – Filinov is obviously peeved about what he alleges to be the condescending and generally unfavourable press given to Soviet rock groups in the Western media. He continues:

It's curious that recently in the pages of various publications – *Time, The Washington Post, Christian Science Monitor, Newsweek* and *Melody Maker* – articles have appeared about the development of Soviet popular music. They report that there have been 'festivals' of pop music in Tblisi and Yerevan with concert programmes by Time Machine, Karnival, Kruise and Arsenal. Of course, these comments are written according to the standard recipe. First of all the author remarks with condescension and irony that all this Soviet music is wretched and it holds no interest for Western listeners, because the techniques are primitive and the musical ideas are about ten years out of date. This is followed by a complimentary part in which it is maintained that there are some 'good ones', in so far as the volume of their music 'shakes the foundations'. The real content of the work is therefore cynically perverted.

The aim of these lies is twofold. The Western public, of course, must be convinced of the successes of bourgeois ideology and the degeneration of the socialist system of values. But the special services and the propagandistic

225

system controlled by them also anticipate a quite specific reaction in our country denigrating Soviet popular music. . . .

Distressed by the 'tendentiousness' of the Soviet press, Novgorodtsev and others like him try, of course, to present themselves as objective judges of musical taste. In reality, the programmes aimed at the USSR have a very clear-cut bias towards music which is aggressive and corrupting, accompanied by anti-Soviet witticisms. The majority of the most popular performers from abroad which do not fall into this category are not heard, while third-rate heavy metal can be heard all too often. Questions concerning the quality of music are at the bottom of the priority lists of the radio propagandists.

Having criticised the selection of foreign bands which are given air time on Western radio programmes and lamented the unfavourable Western media reports on Soviet rock groups, the author proceeds to berate Novgorodtsev for broadcasting extracts from *The Trumpet Call*.

If the letters I quoted previously are in any way representative of a cross-section of Soviet youth, then any objective assessor must conclude that *The Trumpet Call* had already achieved a considerable measure of success. Not so, according to Filinov. He implies that the lyrics of *The Trumpet Call* are intentionally subversive and are simply disguised as religious propaganda:

The remarkable story of the group Trumpet Call is made much of by Seva Novgorodtsev. At home in Leningrad this group is not popular. The musicians play badly and their ideas are banal. Alexander Barinov*, the leader of the group, decided to seek publicity and recorded a cycle of songs on religious

* Valeri's patronymic is Alexandrovich, hence the mistake over his Christian name.

themes. A tape was sent to the BBC★ and before long Seva Novgorodtsev, absolutely overcome, is making out that this dreadful work with its wretched text is the greatest achievement in the field of music. Well, what of it? Pay someone for lying and he'll deliver the goods.

That's what the prophets of the Western musical waves expect from our music – sermons on 'alcoholic themes', undisguised vulgarity, rapturous descriptions of the attributes of the 'sweet life' and a good dose of religious propaganda. And those who swallow this bait play into the hands of our ideological opponents who harm our young people's native music and sow poisonous seeds about a way of life alien to our own society in their uninformed minds.

For us, Soviet people, such a culture is unacceptable. . . .

Filinov certainly will not have won over many of his readership through this article. On the contrary, young people's curiosity will have been aroused by the mention of the Leningrad group. Finally, of all the letters which Valeri and Sergei received in response to Seva's broadcasts and passed on to the West, only one writer was critical of Seva. For the majority of young Soviet listeners he is a hero.

When the article appeared in September 1984, Valeri had already been in prison under investigation for six months. Some Western observers surmised that the reference to Valeri and *The Trumpet Call* in the newspaper at that particular time was an indication that he would shortly be brought to trial. It is sometimes the case that trials of political or religious dissidents are preceded by slanderous attacks on the individuals concerned in the media, intended to arouse public antipathy towards them.

★ This, in fact, is untrue. A tourist brought out a tape and subsequently it was made available to the media in the UK.

In the event it was to be another two months before the trial finally took place. In order to describe the events leading up to it, we must return to March 1984 when a friend, just back from a visit to Leningrad, reported the disturbing news that Valeri and Sergei had gone into hiding.

Although over the past year a great deal of information has become available about the investigation and the trial, inevitably there are contradictions, inconsistencies and gaps in the story it is impossible to give the full facts here. Readers will have to form their own opinion about what happened on the basis of the information which follows, most of which is taken from individuals and official Soviet pronouncements.

In March 1984 Valeri and Sergei both left home, having said goodbye to their wives and children. Both Nina and Tanya believed that their husbands were going 'underground' in order to work secretly on a musical project in connection with the Trumpet Call group. Valeri and Sergei had, in fact, taken a firm decision to try to leave the Soviet Union by crossing the state frontier into Finland somewhere in the Murmansk region, about 500 miles north of Leningrad.

It later transpired that Nina did in fact know that Sergei's 'secret work' was to be on the other side of the Soviet frontier, but Tanya knew nothing about the planned attempt to cross the border.

According to Valeri, they intended to make two recordings in Finland and then return to their homes in Leningrad. It was impossible to make these in their own country because, as active Christians, they were both being persecuted. Only the constant harassment of the last two years can explain such wild enterprise. Valeri was to testify later to this, stressing that the main reason why they took such a risk was because of the persecution they had endured as a result of their religious activities with the rock group, the Trumpet Call. A summons from the Leningrad Procuracy warning them not to spread slanderous fabrications defaming the Soviet social and state system was received by Valeri on 30 January 1984. This had prompted their action.

Another factor which undoubtedly influenced their decision was the refusal of their application in December 1983 for official permission to leave the Soviet Union with their families, on the grounds that there was no legal basis to grant their request.

Valeri managed to get hold of a Finnish map of part of the border area and from it he drew his own sketch map with a planned route across the frontier. Both men assembled various items of equipment including home-made skis, ski suits, warm clothing, foodstuffs, compasses, English-Finnish and Russian-Finnish phrase books.

They left home on 2nd March and travelled by train in the direction of Murmansk. On 3rd March they arrived at Loukhi which is about 100 km east of the frontier zone. When they realised that they were being followed, they decided to abandon their attempt and return to Leningrad. According to Valeri's plans, the route to the frontier was to start near Sofporog inside the frontier zone. However, they were unaware that entry into the town of Kestenga from which they hoped to reach the frontier zone was controlled by special passes. This called for an on-the-spot change of plan which was reinforced by the fact that the locals had noted the presence of two strangers. The first train from Loukhi was going north, towards Murmansk and not back to Leningrad. They decided to board this train and then get out at another station further up the line and from there to return to Leningrad. Sergei had 80 roubles which they had earlier agreed to designate for return tickets to Leningrad in case of a change of plan. They decided to get out at Knyazhaya, one stop before Kandalaksha, because they guessed that if they were still being followed, they were less likely to be detained in a small place such as Knyazhaya than a sizeable town such as Kandalaksha.

Leaving the train at Knyazhaya at about 9 pm. they went into the station's empty waiting room to wait for the

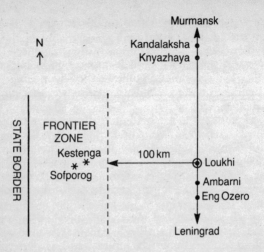

Leningrad train. The ticket office clerk had told them that tickets were not available until one hour before the departure of the train, and so without tickets, they lay down on the benches and went to sleep.

At about midnight, three militia men entered the waiting room. They asked for Valeri's and Sergei's documents. The two men showed their passports. Valeri was asked where he was going. He replied, 'Leningrad'. After checking the documents the militia left the room, one of them saying, 'It's not them'. Five minutes later they returned and again asked to see their documents. Valeri and Sergei were then taken to the police station at Zelenoborsk. Two hours later a Leningrad KGB officer arrived and interrogated Sergei. This clearly demonstrates that the two men had been followed from the time they left Leningrad as it would have taken the officer much longer than two hours to reach Zelenoborsk if he had been travelling from there.

Valeri and Sergei were then taken by car to a special detention centre in Kandalaksha. A senior investigator accompanied them. He asked Valeri where he had been going. Valeri again replied, 'Leningrad'. At the detention centre the interrogation began (presumably in the early hours of the morning). It appears that the investigator, Shelimov, behaved decently and was friendly. Realising that the equipment which he and Sergei had had with them was clear proof of their intention to cross the frontier, Valeri made a frank statement of the facts. Valeri stated that he and Sergei had been forced to take this drastic step because of persecution. He said that the thought – and it was only a thought – had come into his mind that they should travel back south from Loukhi to Ambarni and from there go to the West. However, this thought flashed into his mind only for a second because he knew that it was stupid and that it would be impossible. The investigator offered him tea and 'like a kindly uncle' asked him to write everything down. When Valeri said that he thought he ought to write down that he had changed his mind about crossing the frontier, the investigator pointed out that as there was no tangible proof of this, there was no point in recording it. Valeri was very tired and disorientated and the investigator seemed trustworthy. In reality, he used his professional skill to make Valeri put together a document to his own disadvantage.

What then did the Soviet authorities make of Valeri's and Sergei's evidence and what was their version of the events which led to the arrests? The bill of indictment read at the trial claimed that the two men, discovering at Loukhi that special permits were required to enter the frontier zone and fearing that they were being followed, decided to change their original plan and attempt a border crossing via a different route. It further stated that they travelled by train to Knyazhaya and that from there they intended to travel south to Ambarni or Engozero in order to continue on their planned route to the frontier and to cross it illegally. It claimed that, despite their wish to carry out this plan, they were prevented from doing so because they were arrested at Knyazhaya station on 4th March. In other words, the investigation concluded that there was no sense in which Valeri and Sergei decided voluntarily to abandon the attempt and that they simply dreamed up this version of events as an excuse to evade responsibility for their criminal action.

Later, when it became clear just how the evidence Valeri had given to the investigator had been distorted in order to prove his guilt, he declared a hunger strike. This began on 18 April and he continued for 23 days until 11 May. Valeri also appealed three times to the Procuracy of the USSR explaining the circumstances of the case and how he had been deceived. He asked the Procuracy to take up his case and was advised at the end of May that the latter would control the pre-trial investigation.

Valeri repeatedly asked the prison authorities to inform his wife about what had happened, but his request was ignored. Obviously the authorities did not want any information to leak out to the West too soon and so Tanya and Nina were kept in total ignorance about the arrests for four weeks.

Valeri and Sergei were held in prison in Murmansk for about a month before being transferred to the KGB prison in Voinov Street in Leningrad. During this time they shared cells with a number of prisoners who had been arrested on criminal charges. These men subsequently gave evidence against Valeri and Sergei during the investigation and at the trial.

Finally, on 3rd April groups of KGB and militia arrived simultaneously at the homes of Valeri and Sergei to search them. They also visited three other families in Leningrad who were in some way connected with the two men. The searches lasted from eight am until four pm. All religious literature, personal correspondence and photographs were confiscated. The officers said that these were 'in connection with the cases of Barinov and Timokhin who were arrested in Murmansk on 4th March and charged with attempting to cross the border illegally'. Only then were Tanya Barinova and Nina Timokhina informed that their husbands had been brought to Leningrad and were being held in the KGB prison at Voinov Street.

In the next few days several friends and relatives were

called in for questioning by the KGB, including Nina, her father, Sergei's father, Tanya and her mother. Officials informed them that they were questioning everyone whose names and addresses were found in Barinov's possession. Over the period of the investigation, which was to last nine months, more than sixty young people were interrogated. The questions they were asked had nothing to do with the attempted border crossing. What the KGB wanted to know was who were the members of the Trumpet Call group, how they recorded *The Trumpet Call* and where the equipment which they used was located. None of this information was forthcoming.

In fact a great deal of time and attention was devoted, both during the investigation and at the trial, to exposing the fact that both men had been involved in 'anti-social' activities because they had maintained contacts with 'anti-Soviet organisations' abroad and smuggled slanderous information to them about the position of believers in the USSR. Plainly, the KGB were interested, not in the attempted border crossing, but in the activities of the Trumpet Call group.

What were prison conditions like for Valeri and Sergei? They were kept apart and were therefore unable to offer each other moral support. Almost certainly they would have been subjected to long and exhausting interrogations and at such times mental fatigue often leads to a loss of rational thought, to confusion and despair. Valeri was also suffering physically because of the effects of his hunger strike.

Frequently in the initial stages of a criminal investigation, minimal sentences or freedom are offered in exchange for collaboration with the KGB. In some instances the interrogators ruthlessly exploit the conditions in the investigation prisons to break the prisoners' wills and force them to make a public confession. Valeri and Sergei were put in cells with common criminals. These may have been bribed or given some kind of concession in return for beating up Valeri and Sergei in order to lower their morale.

Other physical and psychological techniques are used to break a prisoner's will and obtain a confession. There have been cases where neuroleptic drugs have been administered in order to 'change' a victim's personality and extract a confession.

This is believed to have happened in the case of Father Dmitri Dudko, an outstanding Russian Orthodox priest and gifted preacher, who exercised an effective pastoral ministry among young people. In the mid-1970s he used to hold open 'question and answer sessions' at the end of the liturgy at the Church of St Nicholas in Moscow where he was priest. Young people flocked to hear him. As his popularity increased, he was subjected to constant harassment which took the form of threats of imprisonment for his whole family, the break-up of meetings at his home and finally an attempt on his life, from which he narrowly escaped with two broken legs.

He was arrested on 15th January 1980, then aged 57, and six months later in June the Soviet current affairs programme, *Vremya* (Time), televised Fr Dmitri reading a statement admitting to 'systematic fabrication and dissemination abroad of anti-Soviet materials'. He then answered a number of leading questions posed by an interviewer who was introduced as a journalist, but whose full name was not revealed. On the following day Fr Dmitri was allowed to return home. Friends of Fr Dmitri who saw the programme were surprised by his apparent good health, his total calm and his radiant smile as he admitted to charges which could result in seven years' imprisonment and five years' exile. But in early July a reliable source in the Soviet Union reported that Fr Dmitri was in a state of deep depression and had lost more than forty pounds in weight.

In the case against Valeri and Sergei, it was obvious from the start that the two men would be found guilty of attempting to cross the Soviet frontier. Valeri and Sergei admitted that this had been their *intention*, but denied any guilt because they had given up the attempt. What would have constituted a victory for the authorities in their case would have been some kind of refutation or renunciation of their religious activities, in particular their association with the Trumpet Call group. They would then have been discredited in the Soviet media, lost support among Soviet youth and the confidence of their admirers in the West.

Prisoners in the USSR are not permitted to see their relatives before they are brought to trial, but they may receive food parcels. Tanya was informed that she could take five kilograms of food to the prison every first Wednesday of the month. However, when Tanya arrived at the prison with her parcel at the beginning of June, she was informed that Valeri had been transferred three weeks earlier to the psychiatric ward at Hospital No. 5 in Lebedev Street. When she demanded to know why she had not been informed, the prison administrators said they had 'forgotten' to tell her. The Soviet authorities, as well as punishing 'offenders', knowingly inflict suffering on innocent relatives. They refused to convey Tanya's parcel to the hospital. A week later, Valeri was transferred back to the KGB prison. During the course of the criminal investigation he was given six psychiatric examinations. Each time he was certified as being in sound mental health.

During the trial the judge constantly suggested that Valeri might be psychologically disturbed. Valeri was therefore forced to inform the court that in 1983 he had been subjected to four psychiatric examinations in hospital and at outpatient clinics and that in 1984 after he had been imprisoned, he was again subjected to regular hospital examinations which lasted a whole month. The professional opinion on the results of all of these examinations concluded that Valeri was completely normal. Valeri stated that the commission of experts who formed this judgement was acquainted with the stipulations of the criminal code and was warned that if it formulated a false diagnosis it would be answerable before the law.

So when these allusions were made by the judge to his mental instability, Valeri told the court that if they wanted to send him for the seventh time to a psychiatric hospital then the commission of experts would automatically be held responsible for a false diagnosis.

In 1983 the Soviet authorities came very close to shutting Valeri away in a mental hospital indefinitely. Now, at the time of the trial, it was expedient not to declare him mentally abnormal. Here is clear evidence of the cynical manipulation of psychiatry for political purposes.

In the Soviet Union criminal investigations are supposed to be completed within six months of arrest and Tanya was therefore expecting the trial to take place at the end of August. If detention is to be extended beyond six months, special permission must be sought from senior legal officials in the State prosecutor's office. Tanya's main concern at that stage was to raise money to hire a defence lawyer for Valeri. The disadvantaged are doubly penalised. Tanya knew she could enlist a good lawyer only by raising a lot of money or being able to offer goods in kind. At that time she was working in a branch of the electrical photographic industry and earning 108 roubles per month (approximately £100). This was barely sufficient to cover basic living costs and to buy food for the family, but she had managed to put aside 20 roubles towards a lawyer's fee. She urgently needed a further 500 roubles. Tanya's flat was kept under close surveillance during this whole period and people could only visit her by slipping into her home late at night. Telephone calls to the West were out of the question, both from the point of view of security and expense.

During those very difficult weeks of waiting Tanya and the children were supported through prayers offered by Christians, both in the Soviet Union and in the West, and given practical help and encouragement by Christians from other towns who knew and loved Valeri. Tanya's mother stayed with her for part of the time to give support.

August passed without any word of a trial. A rumour began that there was a delay because the authorities could not find enough evidence on which to convict the two men. That may have been wishful thinking, but in the light of what followed there was probably some truth in it.

On 16th September Filinov's article appeared and this, as mentioned earlier, was taken as an indication that the trial was imminent. It finally took place from 20th to 23rd November 1985.

On 20th November Nina and Tanya and one or two other relatives went to the Leningrad City Court, but no-one could tell them in which room the trial was taking place. Eventually they found the courtroom by following a television cable from the entrance. They arrived fifteen minutes late and the room was already bristling with KGB officials. Other friends and relatives of Valeri and Sergei were refused entry on the first day, even though it was supposed to be an 'open' trial.

It is very common for this to happen in the Soviet Union when those standing in the dock are considered to be political or religious 'dissidents'. Frequently local workers – from the nearest factory or office building – will be given a day off work in order to attend a trial during which they are instructed to ridicule and jeer at the defendant. In some cases where prisoners have endured months of interrogation, brutal treatment at the hands of the prison guards or fellow prisoners, fatigue, poor diet and the pain of separation from loved ones, to enter such an atmosphere of hostility and mockery can be the final blow which breaks their will and causes them to recant.

It had taken several months of 'work' on Sergei before his will was finally broken. His confession amounted to admitting that he had done wrong by playing Christian music and preaching. Sergei also gave a television interview to Soviet journalists in which he denounced Valeri's contacts abroad.

An observer at the trial said that Sergei hung his head like a miserable dog and could not look Valeri in the eyes. My own guess is that the KGB played on Sergei's concern for his family – his young wife and two children under five years of age – to whom he was absolutely devoted and told him things would be worse for them if he did not comply with their wishes. This incident can only serve to deepen our compassion and love for Sergei and others like him. We must pray for them, remembering Peter's transformation into one of the greatest saints of the New Testament Church after he had denied his Lord.

Here I should add a word of testimony from one of Father Dmitri's 'spiritual children' which puts this apparent tragedy into perspective:

> Father Dmitri's recantation is his last and, possibly, most important lesson to us all. . . . The earth did not cease to rotate around the sun after Galileo recanted . . . and so the truth preached by Fr Dmitri remains. This truth of the Holy Bible which he brought to me and of which nobody will ever be able to rob me. It will continue to warm my heart for as long as it beats in my breast. . . .

Valeri's own reaction to Sergei's conduct was typically charitable:

> 'I was surprised that Sergei did this, but it seems to me that he was simply tricked by the KGB. Sergei did not say anything about our group, about its members, about the equipment we used . . .'.

There is no shortage of information available in the West to demonstrate the true nature of Soviet justice, written both by and about people who have been on trial in the Soviet Union, some of whom have subsequently emigrated or been expelled. For example, the transcript of the 1966 trial of Pastors Georgi Vins and Gennadi Kryuchkov in *Faith on Trial in Russia*, by Michael Bourdeaux (Hodder & Stoughton, 1971), illustrates that not only did the judge refuse to allow the defendants to make a proper case, but he even exhausted them physically by compressing the whole trial into two days, totalling over twenty hours in the courtroom.

238

The trial of Valeri and Sergei proved no exception. During it Valeri asked for permission to read out the three letters which he had earlier written to the Procuracy of the USSR in order to better present his case, but the judge categorically refused.

There are numerous inconsistencies in the indictment as compared with available information on the results of the investigation and what was actually said at the trial. I will give just a few examples of the contradictory 'evidence' presented to the court.

In the indictment it was claimed that witnesses A.V. Popov, V.A. Savichev, V.M. Krasavtsev, N.S. Yelagin and others who were being held in detention with Sergei and Valeri during the period 4th to 21st March in Murmansk declared that the two men had had an opportunity to talk to each other. The witnesses also claimed that the accused consulted with them about how they should conduct themselves during the investigation and that they agreed to stick to their version of the events, namely that they had given up the attempt to cross the border voluntarily.

Savichev further claimed that Valeri had declared his intention to make another attempt to leave the country illegally. Barinov, he alleged, having found out that Savichev lived in Murmansk, inquired about conditions at the frontier and asked him to annotate a sketch map of a particular region of the frontier zone.

Yet persons present at the trial reported that another witness, Yelagin, who had shared a cell with Sergei, declared on the witness stand that Valeri and Sergei had had no contact with each other while in prison and that at Loukhi they had both firmly intended to return to Leningrad. The judge asked Yelagin about the evidence he had given to the investigator, which plainly contradicted what he said at the trial, and about the protocol of the investigation which he had signed. Yelagin replied that there had been no protocol. He stated that a KGB agent, the investigator, Kachkin, got the witnesses together in one cell where they had a chat, laughed and joked. Then they brought Yelagin a paper (the protocol of the interrogation) which he signed without reading because, as he himself stated, 'if they want to imprison you they will do it anyway'.

Popov also gave evidence at the trial, which was disputed by Valeri who asserted that Popov simply made things up as he went along. The evidence he gave during the investigation differed from that given during the trial. After he had testified, Popov stated that the court had no right to question him because on more than one occasion he had received head injuries and had suffered loss of memory and had been placed on the register of psychiatric patients. The facts about his psychiatric illness were given in the documents relating to his own case and he maintained that the investigator, Kachkin, should have known about them.

Valeri protested strongly against the evidence given by Krasavtsev, whom he described as a thief and a recidivist. He also claimed that another of the witnesses, a man named Lyakh, twice sentenced for robbery, had given false testimony against him and in return the KGB had deferred his three-year sentence. Finally there was Savichev, who had three convictions for hooliganism and using a knife and had twice been imprisoned. Even the judge commented that this sentence – a total of four years – was very short. Was a mild sentence his reward for giving false testimony? Savichev's evidence runs contrary to Valeri's, who, while still in prison in Murmansk, wrote to the Presidium of the USSR renouncing his citizenship and asking for official permission to leave the Soviet Union with his family. Valeri explained to the court that he was proud of being Russian, but that as a Christian, Marxist-Leninist philosophy was both alien and unacceptable to him for one reason – it denies the existence of the Creator, Almighty God. 'Therefore it is better that I should be reviled by the Soviet people than to play the hypocrite and live comfortably . . .'.

While he was on hunger strike in April, Valeri was visited by an official from OVIR (the visa office) in Leningrad and informed that he had the right to renounce his citizenship, but would be permitted to leave the Soviet Union only after he had served his sentence.

The investigator claimed that Valeri and Sergei, having discovered that it was impossible to carry out their plan from Loukhi, decided to change the route and to travel to Engozero or Ambarni and try from there. Yet, logically if they really had intended to do this, they would not have travelled north from Loukhi towards Murmansk, but south to the next station on the line which was Ambarni (see map).

In defence Valeri listed a number of points to attest his innocence: Valeri's and Sergei's actions themselves testified to their innocence. The fact that they left Leningrad with their equipment speaks for itself. They left home with one thought in mind – to reach their starting point somewhere in the area of Sofporog and from there to attempt to cross the frontier and the state border. They admit that their intention could be regarded as unlawful. But from Loukhi they did not proceed to Sofporog. They did not travel so much as one metre from the main Leningrad-Murmansk railway line in the direction of the frontier zone and their hasty retreat proved that they had decided not to carry out their criminal intention. It was an *intention* not an *act*.

The fact that they were peacefully sleeping in the waiting room showed that they were not then planning any criminal action, but were waiting for the train to Leningrad. Valeri expressed the opinion that the court should not judge people's intentions, but actual crimes.

However, the charges against the two men (preparing or attempting to commit a crime and illegal crossing of the frontier – Articles 15 and 83 of the RSFSR Criminal Code) were upheld and Valeri and Sergei were sentenced to 2½ and 2 years' ordinary regime camp respectively.

During his final defence speech Valeri stated: 'I am on trial for being a Christian'. He announced that he would go on hunger strike until justice was done or until he and his family were allowed to emigrate. He asked for prayer support from fellow Christians for himself and his family. Valeri claimed both at the time of the trial and later that he had been sentenced, not on the basis of a court examination, but of a crudely fabricated bill of indictment.

The period of detention runs from the day of arrest, so at the time of writing both men have already served nearly a year and a half of their sentence.

My own view is that Valeri and Sergei weakened their position by their actions, but they had endured a great deal at the hands of the KGB and I believe they were desperate. As stated earlier, the authorities had decided early in 1983 that they must stop Valeri's evangelistic work and prevent him from having contact with foreigners – it was simply a question of finding the right time and a suitable pretext on which to convict him. There is no sense in which the two men can be said to have been guilty of crime for which they were sentenced – unless it be an Orwellian 'thought crime'. They were in fact tried for the way in which they lived out their Christian faith, just as Valeri said. If the Soviet Union abided by the Helsinki Agreement, which it signed in 1975, Valeri and Sergei would have been allowed to emigrate.

At the time of the trial Valeri was physically very weak. Although he had had over seven months to recover from the effects of his previous 23-day hunger strike, he had endured considerable mental and emotional strain and had existed on meagre prison rations, supplemented by the food parcels provided by Tanya, not all of which he received. Relatives at the trial were struck by his frailty, his gaunt figure and pale complexion. During his second hunger strike immediately following the trial, the prison authorities force-fed him through the nose.

On 28th November, five days after the trial had ended, Valeri suffered a heart attack. He had had no history of heart ailments. Tanya was permitted to see him for one hour on 29th November, but a guard remained in the room so that their conversation could be overheard. Valeri's appearance gave Tanya cause for great alarm. There was no evidence that he had received any medical treatment. Despite the heart attack, Valeri continued his hunger strike for a total of 40 days. Tanya, apparently unaware that Valeri had decided to continue this form of protest, went to the prison on 5th December to deliver a parcel of food, but it was refused.

The day after the trial ended, 24th November, an article entitled 'The last frontier' by E. Bistunov, was published in the Leningrad evening newspaper, *Leningradskaya Pravda*.

Predictably, the article begins with moralising about those who overstep the accepted norms of Soviet society and their accountability before the law. Soviet journalists have at least to pretend that there is a system of justice in the Soviet Union which is upheld for the good of the collective. The article begins:

> The words *gran* [border, brink, edge] and *granitsa* [frontier, limit] have the same root. In the criminal case which we shall discuss here, these words turned out to be closely linked and not only because of their derivation. The real point about the meaning of the two words is their link with one incontestable truth – overstepping the acceptable boundaries of Soviet morality, the norms of our socialist way of life is often accompanied by lawbreaking. This leads to accountability before the law.

Bistunov proceeds to his main point – a character assassination of Barinov and Timokhin:

> Valeri Barinov and Sergei Timokhin who were present at the Leningrad City Court the other day had always been good-for-nothing scoundrels. They grabbed whatever they could for themselves and had no scruples about the methods they used. They did not burden themselves with honest work. They habitually told lies and deceived others.

> Even when at school, Barinov could not be kept in

check by his teachers or his relatives. His aunt was concerned about her nephew. By her own admission it was she who, in the hope of saving his 'lost soul', advised Valeri to turn to God. To her surprise, he seized upon the idea. . . .

The other defendant, Sergei Timokhin, like Barinov, did not distinguish himself at school and was not known for making progress or for diligence. His only enthusiasm was rock music. His parents, clutching at a straw, decided to make the most of their son's one enthusiasm: 'Let the child go to music school and develop his talent'. But in the family, in order not to upset themselves or their son, they tried not to talk about the fact that their great, strapping son – a head taller than many of his fellow pupils – was distinctly diffident about doing any work whatsoever. He got into a music school, but after two months' study he left. Professional technical school did not satisfy him either. Over a period of almost six years after he had finished his training (specialising in tailoring) Timokhin changed jobs nine times. According to his understanding, his real life nowadays was not work, but his hours of leisure. Play the tape recorder to your heart's content, go out with your friends, swop recordings of pop music – songs by the 'stars', the idols who rise and fall according to the whim of fashion.

Bistunov claims that Valeri, following his 'conversion', got to know believers of different denominations, but decided that it would be most advantageous for him if he joined up with the Baptists. In order to gain a foothold among believers, Valeri was baptised by full immersion and became a member of the registered Baptist Church in Leningrad. He then, apparently, had to determine whether to establish 'brotherly relations' with the registered or the unregistered Baptists:

The problem was not easy to resolve, but Barinov

managed it without giving himself too much difficulty. He decided to be friends with both. After all, what difference does it make if you believe neither in God nor the devil? By that time, he had already learnt how to use the name of the Almighty as a cover for anything, any sin, any corrupt practice.

He then explains that Valeri and Sergei, despite the 14-year difference in their ages, became bosom friends and that, motivated by conceit, tried to think of ways of drawing attention to themselves. Barinov, apparently, invited his 'young friend' to the prayer house, then dragged him off to a meeting of the unregistered Baptists, then to the Orthodox church and finally to a Roman Catholic church. But in addition to these regular visits to church the two are said to have had close contacts with others who professed quite a different brand of religion:

> In this circle the conversation was about anything, only not about God. . . . A great deal of time was spent on all sorts of rumours and pieces of gossip, and those who had not had time to listen to Western radio broadcasts themselves were given the 'latest news'.

The author then launches into a familiar attack against Western propaganda, full of lies and distortions, which is broadcast to the Soviet Union. Seva Novgorodtsev's name, inevitably, crops up again and Bistunov uses virtually the same hackneyed phrases as Filinov's in his article to describe Seva's role at the BBC: 'A renegade who earns money by slandering his own country'.

The author then refers to a specific occasion in 1982 when Barinov and Timokhin decided to make their presence better known to people outside the Soviet Union. It is at this point that my own involvement, and that of various other Westerners, in the lives of the two men is described. As already mentioned, I was in the Soviet Union in 1982 for one week, and on that occasion I did not go to the Leningrad Baptist Church. It was on my previous visit as a student in 1977 that I attended the church regularly and got to know the Barinov family. Bistunov gets his facts wrong because he alleges that on one of my frequent visits to the Baptist Church in 1982 I gave Valeri a pocket-sized Bible with a slip of paper tucked inside with a message typed in Russian. The message was said to be from an 'anonymous well-wisher' and was supposedly addressed to 'brothers and sisters and all Christians persecuted by godless authorities'. The 'well-wisher' foretold a fraticidal war and the end of the world if Christians tolerated such authorities. At the end of the appeal it was suggested that every opportunity should be taken to send information abroad about the persecution of Christians. Another piece of paper hidden in the Bible revealed that the anonymous well-wisher was, in fact, Keston College, directed by Michael Bourdeaux. This incident never took place and the whole story is a fabrication.

Bistunov goes on briefly to describe Valeri's and Sergei's links with various other foreigners, but concludes that the 'most regrettable' contact was with 'sister Lorna'. I, apparently, inflamed the conceit of the two men by enthusiastically praising their rendering of primitive, self-composed texts. I allegedly bemoaned the fact that with such talent, there were no possibilities to develop further their creative 'egos' and to form a Christian rock group. I told them what kind of repertoire would be likely to attract attention to an impromptu rock group and hinted that I was prepared to publicise the group in the West. My next misdeed was to return to the UK and marry Michael Bourdeaux, thereby linking Valeri and Sergei irrevocably with the work of Keston College. I am supposed to have told them what type of materials were 'needed' by the College.

Bistunov describes, with some accuracy, the reaction of believers to Valeri's music. He claims that it offended their religious sentiments and that they would not allow it to be played in church. He describes an occasion on which Valeri and Sergei tried to present the music in church without previous permission and admits that among the young rock fans who turned up in support, there were some non-believers.

He then claims that various agencies in the West have deliberately created a 'fuss' about 'persecution of believers in the USSR' and made a pact with the hostile Trumpet Call group. For example, Keston College received copies of seditious letters and appeals from the group begging for Western support and passed these on to various anti-Soviet institutions, such as the BBC and Voice of America. The appeals were then broadcast over the airwaves:

Barinov and Timokhin were in seventh heaven. What happiness, what glory! Now the whole world was hearing about them. Now they had someone to intercede for them. Now even with 'outsiders' [a Baptist term for non-believers] as well as with believers, Barinov and Timokhin could speak as inspired by their universal 'calling'.

Finally, Bistunov describes the trial and the evidence presented which led to the two men being convicted. His conclusion, not unnaturally, concurs entirely with that of the Leningrad City Court:

Secretly, and ahead of time, they prepared to cross the border illegally. Barinov and Timokhin 'armed' themselves, not with the Word of God, but with more prosaic items, including material which they could pass off as evidence of 'persecution of the faith' to give to their future hosts in the West. Timokhin, in his time, had been called to account for illegal trading and he had with him a copy of the document relating to this conviction. He had been summoned to an administrative commission and fined ten roubles. A visit to the militia was filed as an example of 'evidence of persecution of the faith'.

Bistunov describes Timokhin's confession as follows:

At the time of the preliminary investigation, Timokhin became aware of many things and there are grounds for hope that he had come to understand the wretched consequences of his way of life and his acquaintance with Barinov. In a written declaration to the investigation, he gave a sober account of the outcome of his links with the anti-Soviet clerical centre, Keston College. . . .

Of Valeri's conduct at the trial he writes:

Barinov remained true to himself. Both during the investigation and at the trial he lied, twisting and turning and stubbornly maintaining the story he had thought up – 'voluntary abandonment of the commission of the crime'. . . .

Bistunov concludes that it was Western ideological opponents of the Soviet Union, organisations such as Keston College, which drove Valeri and Sergei to the edge of the abyss and then over it:

The attempt to cross the border illegally was the last frontier by crossing which they threw down a challenge to the law and placed themselves outside society.

The truth is that on more than one occasion Keston College staff advised Valeri against emigration, warning him that it would be impossible illegally, and legally very difficult; his music would not guarantee him a livelihood in the West (though perhaps now that might not be true); his work as an evangelist was so much needed in the Soviet Union and would probably not be as effective in the West.

Valeri is at present in Corrective Labour Camp No. 27 in the Komi Autonomous Republic, near the town of Ukhta. Eye-witnesses have described the conditions in this camp:

248

The prisoners themselves call this zone 'blood-splattered special'. Here, more than anywhere else, there are, as the prisoners say, 'no limits' – in other words, there are no rules. Murders, brutal beatings and suicides are the order of the day. Moreover, this evil and lawlessness goes on among both the prisoners and the administrators. No prisoner knows what will happen to him, and actions against prisoners can usually be traced back to the 'ments' – the administration – who act on the orders of the KGB.

I have no doubt that in the midst of this physical deprivation and spiritual darkness, Valeri will see the Lord's blessing through his ordeals. His joy and confidence will touch the hearts of both camp inmates and personnel. When he was in the special KGB prison many with whom he came into contact became believers and two were baptised on confession of their faith in Jesus Christ.

From the camp, he has somehow managed to send out a short, handwritten note in English. It is addressed to you and me:

Dear Friends, brothers and sisters in Christ Jesus! I ask you help to my family with material things, because I'm in prison now.

Jesus told to us: 'Bring loads of each other and in such way you will perform the Law of Christ'.*

Let the Holy Name of our Lord Jesus Christ will be praised forever and ever.

Your brother in Christ, Valeri.

* (Galatians 6.2).

Conclusion

This cannot be the end of the story of Valeri Barinov. Even if he fails to survive imprisonment, the impact of his personality, his preaching and his presentation of the gospel through music will live on. Just as some fellow-prisoners with Valeri responded to the call to repentance, so will his music retain its power to move Soviet young people – and possibly some in other countries, too.

More likely he will survive and there will be more chapters to write in the future. However, his chances of doing so depend very much on the support he receives. Prayer for him can and should unite Soviet and Western believers. God has used even Valeri's human failings, as well as his obvious strengths, to make him a more effective evangelist and prayer and concern can enable more people to hear that gospel message. Prayer for Sergei Timokhin, after his experiences at the hands of the KGB, is even more important to help him rebuild his moral strength.

Is there anything else that can be done?

Prisoners and prisoners' families are greatly encouraged and comforted by receiving letters from abroad. Of course, the letters do not always get through to their destination, but such is the bureaucratic nature of the Soviet system that they have to be intercepted and noted at some stage. It is important to let Soviet officials know that Christians all over the world are concerned about the fate of Valeri and his family. Valeri, of course, does read English, but it is best to keep messages short and simple. His camp address is as follows:

169418 Komi ASSR
g. Ukhta, p. Nizhni Domanik
OS 34/27 otr. 14.

Tanya, Zhanna and Marina would also appreciate receiving letters from Christians abroad. Although Tanya knows no English the girls are learning it at school and probably it will not be too difficult for them to find someone who can help translate letters.

The Barinovs' address is:

USSR
g. Leningrad
Pr. Khudozhnikov d.9, k. 2, kv. 74

Nina Timokhina's address is:

USSR
g. Leningrad
Pr. Entuziastov d.30, k. 2, kv. 268

There is also a Prayer Action Campaign which is being run by Danny Smith which includes lobbying politicians and church leaders to act on Valeri's behalf. This resulted in two British Party leaders, Neil Kinnock and David Steel, writing to Soviet leader, Mikhail Gorbachev, urging him to review Valeri's case and allow him to return to his family in Leningrad. ('Party leaders join fight to free jailed Baptist' *Baptist Times*, 9 May 1985). At the first ever 'Liberal Youth Day' organised by Liberal MP, Mr David Alton, which took place on 15 May 1985, a spokesman for the Prayer Action Campaign urged young liberals who had gathered from all over Britain to lobby their local MP to support an Early Day Motion tabled by Mr Alton in support of Valeri. Such action is essential in mobilising public opinion, both at grass roots and at leadership level, to support Valeri morally and spiritually and to inform the Soviet authorities of the concern being widely expressed for him and others in similar tragic circumstances. A campaign package which includes a copy of the original English version of the Trumpet Call is available from Danny Smith at the following address:

> PO Box 80
> Cobham
> Surrey KT11 2BQ

Readers might also like to know that a recreation of Valeri's *Trumpet Call* has been recorded by The Dave Markee Band and is available from Window Records.

The original Russian version of *Trumpet Call* has been released on record in the USA and is available from:

> I CARE
> PO Box 1111
> Franklin
> TN37 064
> USA

Keston College will be publishing updates on Valeri's situation as news becomes known. For information and photographs of Valeri and family please write to:

> Keston College
> Heathfield Road
> Keston, Kent
> BR2 6BA
> England

Lyrics From The Trumpet Call

And He will send out His angels at the last trumpet call and He will gather His elect from the four winds, from one end of Heaven to the other.
Hallelujah Chorus
Deo gratia
The Gospel of the kingdom will be preached throughout the whole world as a testimony to all nations and then the end will come.
This is the trumpet call which announces you about the second coming of our Lord Jesus Christ and about the end of the age.
Christ is coming! Christ is coming!
All through the years of hatred and strife
Through tribulation the troubles of life
The good news of Jesus is with us right now
Today and forever – Its growing power
Cry out, cry out you holy trumpet
Cry out, cry out with all your might
Cry out, cry out you holy trumpet

And warn the people of this plight
Listen you people
Prepare for the glory of Christ
Hear His voice calling
Make sure that your hearts are right
Right – right – right
Closer and closer draws now the day
People! He's coming
To tear down the way
People wake up now – you're all gone to sleep
Prepare and make ready
Hallelujah – Come Lord Jesus
Hallelujah – we are waiting you

* * * *

Look! Look how the world wallows in sin –
Look how evil blossoms all around
Woe! woe to you oh man!
People are lost in the darkness of sin
How much sorrow fills the earth
How many tears are shed each day
Who brought this evil into the world

Men hate each other – where
does it lead
Why is there war – what is the
need
Who is guilty of this sin and
shame
Man oh man you're the one to
blame
This is because right from the
start
You turned from God deep in
your heart
You denied that He's alive
Through sin you killed Him –
Jesus Christ
Where evil reigns love grows
cold
Ah ah ah
Once pure hearts to the devil
sold
Ah ah ah
Filled with lies day by day
Ah ah ah
Can human beings live this
way
The world is filled with death
and sin
Ah ah ah
The devil rules he won't give
in
Ah ah ah
Who is guilty of this sin and
shame
Man, oh man you're the one to
blame
This is because right from the
start
You turned from God in your
heart
You denied that He's alive
And then you killed Him –
Jesus Christ
What can I do? What can I do?
What can I do?
If you're lost and astray –

darkness covers the way
If you're trapped and you
cannot get free
If life laughs at you, fate is
mocking you too, Jesus
waits, He alone has the key
Look up to Golgotha, look up
to Golgotha
His innocent blood flows down
from the cross
Look up to Golgotha, look up
to Golgotha
Your heart will find peace right
there in the Lord
If your soul is downcast
If your strength cannot last
If each day brings you closer
to death
If in your despair
You've said you don't care
Come to Jesus in Him you'll
find rest
Look up to Golgotha, look up
to Golgotha,
His innocent blood flows down
from the cross
Look up to Golgotha, look up
to Golgotha
Your heart will find peace right
there in the Lord
Turn away from all strife
From the struggles of life
From the battles without and
within
Find real strength today
Christ shows you the way
To a new life, a pure life in
Him
Look up to Golgotha, look up
to Golgotha
Your heart will find peace right
there in the Lord
Look up to Golgotha!!

* * * *

On Golgotha is suffering and
shame
But the hangman exalts at
Christ's pain
All alone in His anguish Christ
dies
It's for you that He gives up
His life
See His torment His last dying
breath
He suffers to save us from
death
And groaning with sorrow
untold
He takes on all the sins of the
world
Listen my dear friends
Turn your eyes, turn your
eyes, turn your eyes
On Christ
Don't pass by Turn around
Don't pass by
Who can say how He suffered
for our sake
From His lips there came no
complaint
For He sorrows not for self,
but for us, who uncaring, do
not look at the cross
Is it so my friend can it be true
Are you so blind that you'll
pass by too
Can't you see that He loves you
today
That He's willing to show you
the way
Listen my dear friends
Turn your eyes
Don't pass by, don't pass by,
don't pass by
He suffers for you
Don't pass by

* * * *

Worn down by living

And scarred by sin and shame
Saviour to you I've come
I'm sorry for it all
Saviour to you I've come
I'm sorry for it all
A weight of sorrow on my soul
Suffocation
Take this burden from me now
To you oh Lord I pray
Please don't turn away
Reach out to me and touch my
life
I want to live by you alone
Lord
I want to follow your way
But I'm pleading Lord forgive
me now
But I'm pleading Lord forgive
me now
Forgive, Jesus, Forgive
From depths of darkness, from
chasms of despair
Forgive me Lord cry aloud
I know that I'm a sinner
I'm a sinner
There is nothing good in me
A leper inwardly
But Lord my God to you I've
come
Forgive, forgive me Lord
My Saviour!
The storms of living
Have filled my eyes with tears
To you my Saviour and my
God
To you I've brought my need
Forgive, forgive
Bring life back to my soul
My heart needs joy and peace
The sunshine of your love
My Lord

* * * *

My Jesus – I've come to you
now

Thank you
Have mercy? to me a sinner
Make me clean from all my
  sins by
Your holy blood
I want to be your servant
I want to belong to you all my
  life for ever
Keep me in your Holy hands
  from all kinds of evil
Because I want to live for your
  glory
Oh Jesus My Saviour
Amen
Hallelujah

* * * *

Listen world God speaks to
  you today
Listen world oh please don't
  turn away
Listen world see how sin fills
  the cup and runs o'er
Listen my people the time for
  the judgement draws near
Footsteps we hear
Jesus is here, here He comes
Steps we hear
The end of time is now nigh
Listen world wake up how can
  you sleep
Listen world the prophecies
  are clear
Now is the time for the Saviour
  to come for His church
Now is the time and the Lord
  comes to gather His flock
Footsteps we hear, Jesus is
  here, here He comes, steps
  we hear
The Church a Saviour awaits
Footsteps we hear
Praise to the mission of Christ
Steps we hear
The end of time is now close
Listen world God speaks to
  you today

Listen world oh please don't
  turn away
Listen world wake up how can
  you sleep
How can you sleep
Listen world the prophecies
  are clear

* * * *

Brothers and sisters make
  ready, make sure that your
  lamps are lit
Christ is coming go and meet
  him, in glory the bridegroom
  arrives
Be joyful nation of Christ, Be
  joyful Church the bride
He's coming our loving
  Redeemer, To take us to
  God's side
Oh Lord, oh Lord come near
We need you Lord come near
To you oh Lord we plead
We're waiting come for us

* * * *

Still more time, yeah there's
  more time
Still more room, yeah there's
  more room
Still more time, time to repent
Still more room, room to be
  saved
He is coming
He is coming
Listen you people, listen the
  world He is coming
Praise God – He is coming
He is coming Look at the
  judge go out and meet Him
He is coming, He is coming,
  Hallelujah
Come Lord Jesus
We are waiting here so long
Hallelujah Come Lord Jesus,
  We are waiting here Praise
  God.